THE NATIONAL TRUST
FARMHOUSE
COOKBOOK

THE NATIONAL TRUST
FARMHOUSE
COOKBOOK

LAURA MASON

THE NATIONAL TRUST

Acknowledgements

Many people helped with ideas for this book. First, thanks are due to all who sent recipes, in particular Hazel Relph and people from the Lake District, where local pride is still expressed in good food and firmly rooted in tradition. I apologise to those whose recipes didn't make it into the final book. A huge thank you to Sandy Boyd, who patiently drove me around narrow country roads and provided lots of information and contacts. Other National Trust tenants and personnel who provided information, ideas and sometimes ingredients were Julia Horner, Nikki Exton, Ian and Denise Bell, Mark Russell, Bod Brake, Juliet Rogers and the Well Hung Meat Company. Fionnuala Jay-O'Boyle and Nora Brown at Taste of Ulster were tremendously helpful, and Ben Watson at Riverford Farm Shop also assisted. I'd also like to thank Fiona Quarmby, Beverley Cole and Joe and Emma Roberts. Finally, thanks to family and friends who gave practical help and discussed ideas, especially Ruth Grant, Andy and Angela Davidson, Alison and Steve Mummery, Anne Horn and Stella Hobbs.

First published in the United Kingdom in 2005
as *Farmhouse Cookery* by The National Trust
(Enterprises) Ltd

Revised in the United Kingdom in 2009 by
National Trust Books
10 Southcombe Street
London W14 0RA
An imprint of Anova Books Ltd

Text and recipes © Laura Mason
Copyright © National Trust Books

ISBN: 9781905400812

A CIP catalogue record for this book is available from the British Library.

15 14 13 12 11 10 09
10 9 8 7 6 5 4 3 2 1

Printed and bound by 1010 Printing International Ltd, China
Reproduction by Mission Productions Ltd, Hong Kong

Food photography by Tara Fisher
Home economy by Jane Suthering
Food styling by Wei Tang

This book can be ordered direct from the publisher at the website: www.anovabooks.com, or try your local bookshop. Also available at National Trust shops, including www.nationaltrustbooks.co.uk.

Chapter opening images:
Page 2: Yew Tree Farm, Coniston, Cumbria
Pages 16–17: Asparagus Tartlets
Pages 72–73: Cumberland Sausage in Beer
Pages 132–133: Souffléed Green Pea Pancakes
Pages 158–159: Rhubarb and Ginger Fool
Pages 202–203: Strawberry Shortcake
Pages 270–271: Strawberry and Redcurrant Jam

Contents

Introduction 6
US Equivalent Measures 14

Soups and Light Meals 16
Soups 18
Farmhouse Cookery in Wales 30
Light Meals 34
Farmhouse Cookery in Wessex 36

Hearty Meals 72
Farmhouse Cookery in Cumbria 82
Farmhouse Cookery in Yorkshire 98
Farmhouse Cookery in the Garden of England 116

Sauces, Sides and Vegetables 132
Sauces 134
Vegetables 142
Farmhouse Cookery in East Anglia 154

Puddings 158
Hot Puddings 160
Farmhouse Cookery in Devon 168
Cold Puddings 180
Farmhouse Cookery in Cornwall 184

Teatime Treats 202
Bread, Tea Bread and Scones 204
Farmhouse Cookery in the Peak District 216
Farmhouse Cookery in Northern Ireland 226
Cakes and Biscuits 238
Farmhouse Cookery in Scotland 244
Farmhouse Cookery in the Borders 268

Jams, Preserves and Drinks 270
Farmhouse Cookery in the Marches 278

Farming and Food in the 21st Century 302

Index 312
Bibliography 315
Picture Credits 315

Introduction

This book celebrates two things: the tradition of farmhouse cookery, and the link between landscape and food, especially as it is experienced through food produced by the tenants of National Trust properties. The Trust is more than aristocratic houses; it manages farmland scattered across England, Wales and Northern Ireland. The model farm at Wimpole in East Anglia, the little fields of the Cornish coast, the deer parks of the Welsh Marches, the mountains of Snowdonia and the Lake District fells have one thing in common – they have been shaped over the centuries by food production. Beautiful landscapes may appear to be obvious and eternal combinations of grass, rock and water, but with a few exceptions this is an illusion. Much of their charm comes from precise systems of land use, for instance the distinctive pattern of herb-rich meadows stitched together by grey stone walls which has evolved through sheep- and cattle-raising in Upper Wharfedale, Yorkshire. The seemingly perfect vernacular buildings characteristic of such landscapes – great barns, isolated farmsteads, pleasingly composed hamlets or villages – are products of working on a human scale within the constraints of local materials.

Fontmell Down, Dorset.

Food, either as raw ingredients or in particular recipes, could equally be seen as an expression of locality, of local taste working with available materials.

The original idea behind the recipes given here was to raise awareness of the activities of the Trust's farming tenants in the aftermath of the 2001 Foot and Mouth epidemic. During the epidemic farmers were faced with bans on livestock movements, which cut off a major source of income, while media coverage and closure of footpaths adversely affected tourism, removing another. Some farmers began to market their produce directly, offering personal assurances of welfare standards and traceability. For many farmers this was a direct response to the difficulties imposed by the epidemic and a realisation that they produced interesting foods of excellent quality which deserved better than the small sums offered by the government during the emergency. Livestock farmers also had to think creatively when their farms became overstocked due to restrictions on the movement of animals.

As far as farmhouse cookery is concerned, it could be argued that farmers, like other people, rely on supermarkets for food. In the 21st century, the idea of farmhouse cookery embraces a series of vague notions involving Aga cookers and bunches of cut herbs gathering dust. Farmers' wives, diminishing in numbers along with farmers themselves, are more likely to be working in towns several miles away than making cheese and butter, raising poultry or preserving fruit. The cookery traditions of the countryside were gradually eroded by urbanisation in the 19th century, and then bastardised by the expediencies of rationing during the Second World War. They have been further diluted by supermarkets and disowned by most cookery writers.

Despite this, there are people keeping ideas about traditional cookery and baking alive, and developing new sources of income for fragile, dwindling communities in the face of globalisation. Some of these people regularly cook recipes that have been used by their families or in their region for generations; others develop new ideas within the constraints of what their land produces and their own feelings of what is appropriate. Some of their recipes and ideas appear in this book. In addition, I have drawn on my own background as the child of a farming family. For other ideas, I have consciously looked back to before the Second World War. At this time several people made an effort to record traditional cookery, and I owe a debt to the work of Florence White, particularly *Good Things in England* (1932), the Women's Institute (W.I.) and Mrs Arthur Webb (who doesn't record her own Christian name), who toured the country in her car in the 1930s, writing columns for *Farmers Weekly*. The work of more recent writers such as Theodora Fitzgibbon, Jane Grigson and Bobby Freeman has also provided ideas. Much of what was recorded in the 1920s and 1930s was of the 'good plain cooking' school – fine in the hands of good plain cooks supported by knowledgeable gardeners and tradesmen, but risky when practised by plain bad cooks using poor ingredients. The plainness was partly a response to the poverty which much of the population, urban and rural, endured during the 19th century; there is much evidence that earlier English food was both rich and well seasoned. At its best, the effect is a rustic simplicity of the type much admired when encountered in France or Italy, but belittled at home. I aimed for a balance between recipes still meaningful because they are rooted in a particular region and others which focus on local products. Some recipes have been left strictly alone, while for others I have given more elaborate seasonings or altered their presentation, though not too much, as this is not a book of restaurant cookery, but nor is it a recipe museum. Tradition is not tradition unless it changes subtly, and some much-loved and symbolic foods, such as fruit cakes, have little to do with our landscapes, yet they preserve memories of distant fashions, novelties and rituals in an edible form which has altered gradually over time.

Speckled and Black Rock hens at Low Sizergh Farm in Kendal, Cumbria.

The meals and dishes eaten in farmhouses have their own internal logic. This is how it appeared to one who grew up on a dairy farm in the Yorkshire Dales. You arose between five and six and had a cup of tea and a small bite to eat before getting on with the first milking. After two or three hours, you adjourned for a more substantial breakfast of porridge or cereal, bacon, eggs and toast or teacakes. The day's agenda was set by the season, but always involved much routine work, and was punctuated by dinner, the biggest meal. Everyday dinners required good-tempered dishes such as stews and hotpots which looked after themselves in a low oven, a necessity in busy households where most people were outdoors. These were made in large quantities for workers whose exact numbers were sometimes unknown until the table was being set. They are also filling, another necessity when the company has been working in the open air in all weathers. Work in the afternoon depended partly on the season, with a lighter workload during the worst of the winter weather. Tea, in the late afternoon or early evening, after the second milking, usually brought the day to a close. Tea was important, as it came at a time of day when one could generally expect to relax. Everyday tea was a miscellany of soup or eggs or cold meat or pies or salads, bread and lots of cakes. Baking to fill the cake tins was a major activity in a farmhouse kitchen. Special teas, for birthdays and social occasions such as club meetings or cricket matches, included numerous different types of sandwiches and fancy cakes.

Naturally this schedule varied according to the season, family custom and region. The routines of growing grain demand more sustained bursts of outdoor work over several days, but not – as tractors replaced horses – consistently early starts, except at crucial times such as harvest. Raising sheep calls for long hours at lambing time and shearing. What all types of farming still have in common is a reliance on the right weather at the right time and, despite mechanisation, a degree of exposure to the elements. The emphasis on meat, cream, butter and animal fats in many recipes may seem unhealthy but these were the basics to hand, and the calorie-dense dishes reflected the appetites of those spending the best part of the day outdoors. A mango smoothie and plate of salad will not sustain a worker through a chilly day spent sorting sheep on a Lake District fell or drilling seed on the East Anglian fens. The food was not always heavy, however. There were lighter dishes for summer, for special occasions and simply for variety, and some of these are also included. Inevitably, as all cookery writers do, I have picked the best and most interesting recipes. Much of the time food would be plainer – which is as true for, say, rural France as it is for the Yorkshire Dales, but which tends to be overlooked in our culture of easy abundance.

Basic food traditions are national, but have regional nuances. Farmhouse traditions contain numerous variations on the theme of meat and potatoes, on small bread rolls and scones, and cakes large and small. The South West of England has a tradition of using pastry and clotted cream; in the South East of puddings in suet crusts; and Wales of soupy stews and baking on the *planc*, an iron plate suspended over the fire. Baking from the Scottish Borders also featured the iron hotplate, known here as a girdle. The Lake District has a tradition of using brown sugar and spices derived from the West India trade once important to local harbours, while Yorkshire food included oatcakes and oatmeal parkin. Fruit was particularly regional, with emphasis on apples and cider in the South West and East Anglia, orchard fruit generally in Kent, and apples, pears and plums in the West Midlands. The north relied more on gooseberries and rhubarb, with damsons in the Lake District. Most kitchen gardens included potherbs such as leeks, cabbage and onions, but special items such as asparagus and watercress were grown in limited areas. Differences between regions come from cooking methods, availability of ingredients, local tastes and survivals of items that were once the height of fashion but which have been forgotten everywhere except in one small corner of the country.

Most of the recipes require little in the way of special equipment; where this is needed it is specified. Several of the recipes in the baking section call for a piece of equipment known variously as a *planc* (Wales) or a girdle (northern England and Scotland). This indicates a heavy, perfectly flat iron plate or griddle, which was heated directly over a fire. Some hobs come with hotplates that can be used instead – or use a heavy cast-iron frying pan.

Cattle at White Park Bay on the north Antrim coast, Northern Ireland.

Here are a few pointers which will help with some of the recipes.

Yeast is easily, available in dried form. All yeasted recipes in this book have been tested with dried active yeast which is 'started' by adding the required amount to warm, sweetened liquid and leaving it to stand for 10 minutes or so until frothy. The easy blend type, which is mixed with the dry ingredients, works for plain doughs, but I have not found it successful for rich mixtures containing cream, butter or eggs.

Rennet is an enzyme that curdles milk. Originally it was derived from calves' stomachs; the rennet commonly sold now is cultured using microbes and is a vegetarian product. Once opened, store in the fridge. It will lose its strength gradually, taking longer to set milk, so try to use it fairly quickly. Milk for rennetting should be at blood heat, and once the rennet is added do not disturb until set.

For vegetarians, many recipes call for butter, lard or suet. Margarine, block vegetable fat designed for baking and vegetarian suet can be used instead.

Basic shortcrust pastry: the basic rule for shortcrust pastry is to use half the weight of fat to flour. The type of fat used affects the flavour and texture. Lard produces a very short pastry, butter gives a pastry that is less short but has a good flavour. Many cooks favour a mixture of the two. Solid vegetable fat and margarine can both be used for pastry making, but reduced-fat and low-fat spreads are unsuitable.

300g (10oz) flour, mixed with a generous pinch of salt
150g (5oz) butter, lard or butter and lard mixed (this should be well chilled)
6–8 tablespoons cold water

Sift the flour and salt into a bowl. Cut the fat into 1cm (½in) cubes and add to the flour. Rub the fat into the flour until the mixture resembles fine breadcrumbs. Add sufficient water to make a coherent dough, a little more or less may be needed. Shape into a ball, wrap in cling film and put in a cool place for at least 30 minutes to rest before using.

Welsh mountain sheep
on Watkin Path at
Hafod Y Llan farm,
Snowdonia, Wales.

US Equivalent Measures

Dry Measures

1 US cup	50g	1¾oz breadcrumbs
1 US cup	70g	2½oz rolled oats
1 US cup	80g	3oz desiccated coconut
1 US cup	100g	3½oz walnut pieces, icing sugar
1 US cup	120g	4oz white flour
1 US cup	150g	5oz wholemeal flour
1 US cup	175g	6oz mixed peel, sultanas
1 US cup	200g	7oz Demerara sugar, rice
1 US cup	225g	½lb cream cheese
1 US cup	300g	10oz mincemeat
1 US cup	350g	12oz treacle, jam

Liquid Measures

¼ US cup	60ml	2fl oz
1 US cup	240ml	8fl oz
2 US cups (1 US pint)	480ml	16fl oz

Butter, Lard and Margarine Measures

¼ stick	25g	2 level tablespoons	1oz
1 stick (1 US cup)	100g	8 level tablespoons	3½oz

Note: Unless otherwise stated, use plain flour and salted butter; ordinary table salt is fine; black pepper is best freshly ground from a pepper mill. If the peel or zest of lemons or oranges is required, try to find unwaxed fruit. Spoon measures are level unless otherwise stated.

Ashness Farm,
Borrowdale, Cumbria,
a working Lakeland
fell farm with its
16th-century farmhouse.

Soups and Light Meals

Soups

Bubble and Squeak Soup

This is good for showing off the potatoes and cabbage which southern Cornwall grows in vast amounts. The basic Cornish recipe closely resembles Portuguese *caldo verde*. For a vegetarian version, omit the bacon and use a little extra butter.

Melt the butter in a large pan and add the bacon. Cook gently until crisp, then remove and set aside. Add the onion to the fat and cook gently until soft but not brown. Add the potatoes and water. Simmer until the potatoes are soft, then use a potato masher to break them down.

Discard the biggest outside leaves of the cabbage, plus any torn or discoloured bits and the chunkiest parts of the stems. Wash thoroughly and cut the largest leaves in half lengthways. Roll several leaves together in a tight roll and slice finely. Add it to the basic soup. Season well. Cook gently for another 7–10 minutes until the cabbage is tender. Add the cream and serve with a scattering of the bacon pieces in each bowl.

SERVES 6

30g (1oz) butter
120g (4oz) bacon,
    cut into matchsticks
½ medium onion, finely chopped
900g (2lb) maincrop potatoes,
    peeled and cut in chunks
1 litre (1¾ pints) water
200g (7oz) spring cabbage
salt and pepper
100ml (3½fl oz) single cream

Lentil and Caraway Soup

Devised to use stock from cooking ham in cider, this recipe has a pleasing, slightly sour note. Not everyone likes caraway and you may prefer to use cumin instead, which gives a Middle Eastern flavour.

Melt the butter in a large pan. Add the chopped onions, cover and cook very slowly, stirring occasionally – eventually they will begin to catch and turn gold. Add the caraway seeds, stir for a moment, then add the lentils and stock.

Simmer for about 30 minutes: the soup is ready when the lentils are soft. Check the seasoning: it is unlikely to need any more salt, especially if using the ham stock.

SERVES 6

60g (2oz) butter
2 medium onions, finely chopped
1 teaspoon caraway seeds
60g (2oz) red lentils
1.5 litres (2½ pints) stock from the recipe for Ham Cooked in Cider (see page 53), or use a mixture of chicken stock and dry cider

Green Pea Soup

A family recipe originally from Wessex –
Somerset to be precise. This recipe was
recorded by Florence White in the 1930s
but dates from the 18th century.

Bring the water to the boil in a large pan and add 300g
(10oz) of the peas, the mint, celery and the lettuce, plus
the salt and sugar. Cook briskly for 20 minutes, then
put the whole lot through a *mouli-légumes*. Return the
mixture to the pan, add the remaining peas and bring
back to the boil. In a separate pan, melt 30g (1oz) of the
butter and cook the cucumber and onion gently, without
allowing them to brown. After 10 minutes, add to
the soup.

Knead the remaining butter with the flour and drop it in
small bits into the hot soup, stirring well. It should thicken
a little, but don't allow it to boil. Correct the seasoning.
Serve with a little chopped mint scattered over the top.

SERVES 6

850ml (1½ pints) water
300g (10oz) green peas
   (frozen are fine), plus
   an extra 100g (3½oz)
2 sprigs fresh mint or fennel,
   leaves only, plus extra
   to serve
1 stick celery, chopped
½ Cos lettuce, shredded
1 teaspoon salt
1 teaspoon granulated sugar
40g (1½oz) butter
½ cucumber, peeled, cut into
   quarters, de-seeded and diced
½ large onion, finely sliced
1 tablespoon plain flour

Spinach and Sorrel Soup

Market gardens, such as the one at Beningborough Hall, North Yorkshire, produce many unusual vegetables and herbs, including sharp-tasting sorrel, which is good in this soup recipe.

Melt the butter in a saucepan and fry the onion gently until soft but not coloured. Add the spinach and sorrel leaves and allow them to wilt. Stir in the flour, then the stock, and bring to the boil. Liquidise or sieve and return to the pan. Taste and add salt and pepper as necessary and divide between bowls. Mix the horseradish with the cream and serve a spoonful floating on top of the soup in each bowl.

SERVES 4

40g (1½oz) butter
1 medium onion, finely chopped
200g (7oz) young spinach leaves
150g (5oz) sorrel leaves
20g (¾oz) plain flour
350ml (12fl oz) light chicken
   or vegetable stock
salt and pepper
1 teaspoon grated horseradish
2 tablespoons double cream,
   whipped

Spinach Soup

The original 19th-century recipe for this soup, which came from Suffolk, made a tasty but slightly muddy looking purée to be served with suet dumplings. This makes a lighter, elegant green and white soup. Today's consumers might prefer croutons to dumplings.

Sweat the turnips, onions and celery in the butter for 15 minutes. Add the chicken stock and simmer until soft. Put the mixture through a *mouli-légumes* or process to a purée. Return to the pan and add the water. Return to simmering and add the spinach, stirring slowly. Stir in the cream, add the nutmeg and season.

To make the croutons, cut a couple of crustless slices of white bread into 1cm (½in) cubes and fry them in a little olive oil until crisp and golden. Drain well before using.

Pour the soup into bowls and garnish with a few croutons on each serving.

SERVES 6–8

200g (7oz) prepared weight
  of small white turnips, peeled
  and diced
200g (7oz) onions, finely chopped
200g (7oz) celery, finely chopped
knob of butter
600ml (1 pint) well-flavoured
  chicken stock
700ml (1¼ pints) water
200g (7oz) spinach, shredded
50ml (2fl oz) single cream
salt, pepper and nutmeg
slices of white bread, for croutons
olive oil

Stilton and Celery Soup

Stilton cheese production is mostly centred on Leicestershire, to the south-east of the Peak District, but some is made in Derbyshire. Stilton and celery often appeared together on the Edwardian table; since the 1970s the combination has become a modern classic soup.

Melt the butter in a large pan. Add the onion and celery and sweat gently for 30 minutes but don't let them brown. Stir in the flour, then add the chicken stock and milk and simmer for another 30 minutes. Process to give a reasonably smooth texture (the celery will not break down entirely). Return to the pan and add the Stilton. Cook gently for a few minutes, stirring, until the cheese has melted. Taste and correct the seasoning. Serve with a little chopped parsley scattered over the soup.

SERVES 4–6

60g (2oz) butter
½ onion, finely chopped
1 head celery, washed, trimmed
   of any leaves and chopped
30g (1oz) plain flour
400ml (14fl oz) chicken stock
   or vegetable stock
400ml (14fl oz) milk
250g (9oz) blue Stilton, crumbled
salt and pepper
chopped parsley to serve

Hare Soup

There are several different recipes for hare soup in English and Scottish collections. This is a very aristocratic one devised by a 19th-century French chef.

Melt the butter and add the bacon. Fry gently for a few minutes, then remove the bacon to your soup pan. Brown the hare joints in the same fat and add them to the bacon. Stir the flour into the remaining fat, add the wine and stock and scrape up any sediment. Add this to the bacon and hare along with the onion, mace, peppercorns, bouquet and the salt. Simmer gently for at least 1½ hours (an older hare will take up to 3 hours). Strain the soup into a clean pan. Pick over the debris, removing the meat from the hare bones. Cut into small pieces and add this to the soup, plus any bacon bits you find. Discard the remaining debris.

Stir in the redcurrant jelly and bring the soup back to the boil. Add the mushrooms and cook for a further 10 minutes. Serve with a little torn basil floating in each bowl.

SERVES 6

30g (1oz) butter
100g (3½oz) lean bacon, cut
    into matchsticks
1 young hare, or the forequarters
    of a mature one, jointed
1 tablespoon plain flour
400ml (14fl oz) red wine
500–600ml (about 1 pint) good
    beef stock
1 large onion, stuck with
    a few cloves
1 blade of mace and a few
    peppercorns
bouquet garni of parsley, thyme,
    a bay leaf, marjoram, rosemary
    and basil
½ teaspoon salt
2 teaspoons redcurrant jelly
200g (7oz) mushrooms, sliced
fresh basil to serve

Mutton and Barley Broth

A way of using one of the less elegant cuts of lamb or mutton, barley broth is associated with Scottish cookery. The garlic and lemon are not traditional, but they give the soup a lift.

Put the meat in a pan and add the water. Gently bring to the boil and skim off all the impurities. Add the vegetables. Simmer gently for 2 hours, adding a little more water if it seems to be evaporating. Strain the broth into a bowl and allow to cool. Pick the best of the meat off the bones, then discard these and the vegetables. Skim all the fat off the top of the broth. Put the broth in a clean pan with the pearl barley and simmer gently for about 40 minutes or until soft. Add the meat and season with salt and pepper.

Crush the garlic, then mix with the parsley and a little grated lemon zest – just enough to tell it's there. Divide the broth and barley between bowls and add the parsley mixture just before serving.

SERVES 6

1.5kg (3¼lb) scrag end of lamb
  or mutton, chopped
2 litres (3½ pints) cold water
120g (4oz) carrot, scraped
  and sliced
60g (2oz) turnip, chopped
1 medium onion, chopped
4 sticks celery, chopped
60g (2oz) pearl barley
salt and pepper
1 small garlic clove, a little
  chopped parsley and a scrape
  of lemon zest to serve

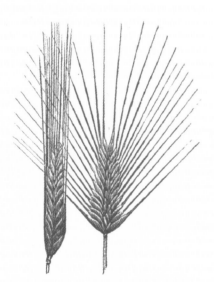

Hotch Potch

This slowly cooked soup-stew is a traditional Scottish recipe which can be traced back to the late 18th century, and might, perhaps, be viewed as a summer version of barley broth. It is the sort of dish that can be left simmering very gently all day on a kitchen range – or nowadays, an Aga. Otherwise, use the lowest possible heat on the hob, or cook in a slow oven. Cookery writers are united in saying that the slower and longer it is cooked, the better.

Put the scrag end of lamb in a soup pot and add the water and a teaspoon of salt. Bring to the boil, skim, cover and cook on a very low heat for at least 1½ hours, preferably longer. Wash, peel and prepare all the vegetables. Cut the turnips and carrots into small neat dice, slice the spring onions into pieces about 1cm (½in) long, peel the broad beans, divide the cauliflower into florets, and slice the lettuce.

Drain the lamb stock off into a bowl and reserve. Lift out the scrag end, pick out any meat and discard the fat and bone. Clean the pan, and put the pieces of meat back in. Skim off and discard any fat that has risen to the surface of the stock, then return the liquid to the pan. Add the diced turnips, carrots, the spring onions and half the peas, and the best end of neck cutlets. Bring back to the boil and continue to simmer gently for at least another 1½ hours. The vegetables should be tender and the meat well cooked through before the final stage.

To finish making the soup, add the remaining peas, the broad beans, cauliflower and lettuce and cook gently for about another 30 minutes until they are all tender. Taste and add salt as you feel necessary.

Serve in soup bowls, putting a cutlet in each, and scatter with chopped parsley and mint before serving.

SERVES 4 GENEROUSLY

about 500g (1lb) of scrag end
  of lamb
1.5 litres (2½ pints) water
3 small white turnips
3 young carrots
6 spring onions
200–250g (7–9oz) broad beans
  (shelled weight)
½ small cauliflower
1 small lettuce
250g (8oz) peas, fresh or frozen
4 best end of neck lamb cutlets
salt
chopped fresh parsley and mint,
  to serve

Cawl

Cawl is a stew-like soup made with lots of vegetables and cheap cuts of meat, such as boiling bacon, ham hock or beef brisket. It was the all-purpose everyday dish of Welsh farming communities, and everybody had their own version (see the following page for more on traditional Welsh recipes and ingredients). It's also impossible to make quickly or in small quantities, but if you want to feed a lot of people on a cold day it is ideal. This recipe is adapted from one used by Bobby Freeman. Like most dishes of this type, it improves with reheating.

Prepare all the root vegetables for the first stage by peeling and cutting them in rough cubes 2cm (¾in) square. Chop the celery.

Melt the fat and brown the beef and ham or bacon, and transfer it to the pan in which you intend to cook the cawl. Next brown the root vegetables and add them to the meat. Add the celery and enough cold water to cover. Bring to the boil, skim, and add the bouquet garni and some pepper (no salt at this stage). Simmer for about 4 hours. At this point, the soup can be cooled and stored overnight if you wish.

For the second stage, remove the meat and carve into neat slices, trimming off any fat and gristle. Return to the soup along with the potatoes and simmer for a further 20 minutes. Taste and add salt and pepper as necessary. About 10 minutes before serving add the cabbage, then the leeks. Serve in deep bowls, making sure each one gets a few slices of meat. Sprinkle with chopped parsley.

SERVES 8

FOR THE FIRST STAGE
2 onions
2–3 large carrots
2 parsnips
1 medium swede or turnip
2 sticks of celery
beef dripping, bacon fat or oil
500–750g (1lb 2oz–1lb 10oz)
    beef brisket
500–750g (1lb 2oz–1lb 10oz)
    boiling bacon, or a ham hock
1 bouquet garni
pepper

FOR THE SECOND STAGE
500g (1lb 2oz) small new
    potatoes, scraped
½ small white cabbage,
    finely chopped
2–3 leeks, thinly sliced
salt and pepper
chopped fresh parsley

You will need a very large pan
or stockpot

Farmhouse Cookery in Wales

Wales is, of course, a separate country with language, customs and, to some extent, food all of its own. From north to south, the country divides into three main areas of superb mountain landscapes: Snowdonia, a mass of shattered volcanic rock cut across by U-shaped, glaciated valleys; the Cambrian mountains, running down the centre, which vary in their ruggedness but are still spectacular, and in the south the high but smooth slopes of the Brecon Beacons – sandwiched, confusingly, between Black Mountain to the west and the Black Mountains to the east. Other smaller mountain areas such as Cadair Idris provide equally stunning scenery. Much of the Welsh coast is undeveloped, varying from flat tidal estuaries such as Llanrhidian Sands, which separate the Gower Peninsula from the mainland, to the rock-strewn beaches of Marloes Sands near Milford Haven.

The north, apart from the Dee estuary and the slate quarries of the Conwy coast, is almost exclusively rural, the landscape moving through the relatively gentle hedged pastures of the Vale of Clwyd to the dramatic lake and mountain scenery of Snowdonia, with tawny and black peaks and ridges fit only for grouse, deer and the hardiest of sheep. South-east from Snowdonia, the Llyn Peninsula points into the Irish Sea, with little bumpy hills above flat, almost treeless fields and a rocky shore. Anglesey, too, is relatively flat, with small fields divided by hedges and boulder walls.

In south-east Wales the landscape is a post-industrial one, where the spoil heaps of the Rhondda and the valleys to the east slowly revert to nature, although the Usk Valley escaped industrialisation and maintains a pleasing landscape of hedged fields dotted with trees. Another strip of industry lies along the south coast between Newport and Swansea. From here westwards the countryside opens out again, reaching into the Gower, which remained one of the most culturally distinct parts of Wales into the early 20th century. And then there is Pembroke, 'little England beyond Wales', settled with the English in Henry VIII's reign, and still showing the legacy in English place names.

Given the mountainous landscape and the high rainfall it is inevitable that grazing sheep and cattle are major occupations. Welsh sheep are small and hardy, some black-woolled or with striped 'badger' faces; Welsh cattle are also black. Although there is a cheese named for the town of Caerphilly, cheese-making ceased to be a Welsh concern for part of the 20th century, when production moved to the Somerset area. The recent revival of cheese-making has affected Wales as much as England, and Caerphilly is now made in the area again; a number of other new-wave cheese-makers work further west, especially in the Pembrokeshire area. Cheese is popular: it is said that the slightly soft, moist texture of Caerphilly evolved to suit the tastes of coal miners, who used it in their packed meals. Welsh rarebits and other dishes involving cooked cheese are also widespread. Butter has long been an important dairy product in Wales; both Welsh butter and Welsh bacon are noted for being very salty.

West Wales, especially the level, fertile fields which chequerboard the Pembroke coast, grows good early potatoes. Leeks, which are one of the national symbols of the country, are used in cookery but attempts to make them into often very good dishes in their own right seem slightly self-conscious, rather than rooted in firm tradition. The south-eastern parts of Wales share the cider and apple tradition of Herefordshire, Worcestershire and Gloucestershire, otherwise fruit was grown only for local or domestic use.

Welsh cookery uses several techniques that are either unique to the country or have been forgotten elsewhere in Britain; simple methods of producing satisfying meals with the ingredients to hand and little more than an open fireplace to cook on. Broths and soups involving many ingredients are typical. The standard dish, *cawl*, includes meat and numerous vegetables to provide broth and a main course from the same pot (see the previous page for this recipe). Another unusual feature is the *planc*, which was originally a flat piece of iron balanced over an open fire. Electrically heated versions can be seen in action in Swansea Market, for baking Welsh cakes. The *planc* was also used for other things – pancakes and pikelets, relatively large loaves made from conventional bread dough, and pastry turnovers filled with fruit, the sugar added after cooking to prevent the juices bubbling out. Until the early 20th century oats were an important cereal in Wales, as in other upland areas of Britain, but the habit of using them to make oatcakes, dumplings, flummery and various drinks seems to have vanished.

Sheep on the Watkin Path at the Hafod Y Llan farm, Snowdonia, Wales.

Broad Bean Cawl

Cawl (see also page 28) is a Welsh dish, halfway between soup and stew. This pretty pink and green soup is based on a harvest-time version. A busy farmer's wife would probably not bother to remove the pale outer skins of the beans, but it is worth the effort.

Cook the bacon gently in the soup pan, just until the fat begins to run. Add the potatoes, turnip, leeks and the water. Simmer gently until the vegetables are soft. Stir in the oatmeal, then add the broad beans and parsley. Cook for about 10 minutes more. Check the seasoning and serve in deep bowls. Some grated Cheshire cheese can be added to top each bowl.

SERVES 4

100–120g (3½–4oz) salty bacon, cut into matchsticks
200g (7oz) new potatoes, scraped and cut into 1cm (½in) dice
1 small white turnip, peeled and cut into 1cm (½in) dice
2 leeks (white part only), sliced
850ml (1½ pints) water
1 dessertspoon fine oatmeal
200g (7oz) broad beans (weight after podding), peeled
2 tablespoons chopped fresh parsley
salt and pepper
Cheshire cheese, grated (optional)

Ulster Broth

A 'visiting' dish, always on the simmer at midday for whoever's around or in the evening for when the family returns home. 'Soup celery' means the leaves – use the leaves from a head of celery if you can't buy this. 'Soup mix' is a mixture of pearl barley, split peas and red lentils, sold in Northern Ireland and some parts of mainland Britain. If you can't buy it, use a third of each of the pulses to make up the weight given here.

Put the stock in a large pan and set over the heat. Add the onion, celery leaves, carrots, chopped parsley and soup mix or pulses, plus a teaspoon of salt and simmer gently for about an hour. By this time the pulses should be cooked. Taste, add more salt and pepper as required and serve with a little fresh chopped parsley in each bowl. This is one of those dishes that tastes even better reheated the next day. A bowl of this soup with a good slice of wheaten bread (see page 206) is a complete meal.

SERVES 6

2 litres (3½ pints) good chicken
    or beef stock
1 large onion, chopped fairly finely
soup celery or 1 handful of
    celery leaves
2 large carrots, peeled and chopped
1 handful of fresh chopped parsley,
    plus extra to serve
120g (4oz) soup mix or mixed
    pulses (pearl barley, split peas
    and red lentils)
salt and pepper

Light Meals

Nikki Exton's Duck Egg Frittata with Spinach and Butternut Squash

National Trust tenant Nikki Exton keeps ducks and devised this recipe to show off their eggs and the vegetables from her Dorset farm. The colours are fantastic, and it tastes good too – duck eggs have a rich flavour. If you can't find duck eggs, use free-range organically produced hen eggs. It is important to cook duck eggs thoroughly.

Put the prepared squash in an ovenproof dish with a little of the butter. Bake at 220°C, 425°F, Gas mark 7 for 20 minutes until just done.

Melt a little butter in a frying pan and add the garlic, then the spinach. Stir it around; the leaves will wilt dramatically. Remove from the heat when soft.

Beat the eggs, add plenty of pepper, the salt and cheese. Stir in the cooked squash, spinach and garlic. Over a high heat, melt the remaining butter in the frying pan. When it begins to foam, pour in the mixture. Stir it a little to begin the cooking process. Then turn the heat down very low and leave to cook gently for 10–15 minutes, by which time the frittata should be mostly set but slightly runny on top. Put the lid on to complete the cooking: it is done when the top is set. Scatter with chopped walnuts. Serve hot or cold, cut in wedges.

1 small butternut squash, seeds, strings and peel removed, cut into 1cm (½in) cubes

40g (1½oz) butter

1 garlic clove, crushed

150g (5oz) spinach, picked over and washed

6 duck eggs, or 8 hen eggs

freshly ground black pepper

½ teaspoon salt

60g (2oz) good-quality Cheddar, coarsely grated

3–4 walnuts, chopped

You will need a large frying pan with a lid

Baked Eggs with Tarragon

This recipe, devised with the produce of some of the National Trust's Dorset tenants in mind, makes an excellent starter or tea-time dish, especially if you have good free-range eggs available (see the following page for more information about typical recipes and ingredients from Wessex).

Mix the cream and tarragon, and season with salt and pepper. Divide between the buttered ramekins. Break an egg into each dish. Bake at 180°C, 350°F, Gas mark 4 for 15–20 minutes until the whites are set but the yolks remain soft.

SERVES 4

125ml (4fl oz) single cream
2 teaspoons chopped fresh
   tarragon
salt and pepper
4 eggs

You will need 4 individual ramekin dishes greased with a little butter

Farmhouse Cookery in Wessex

Wessex became synonymous with Dorset through Thomas Hardy's novels, depicting a deep-rooted rural community remote from the England of industrial cities. Even now, south Dorset – a maze of little valleys winding between spurs with the occasional church of grey stone or flint with a squat little tower – feels far removed from the 21st century. But Wessex is more than just Hardy country. It was the Saxon name for a kingdom that occupied roughly the land now covered by Dorset, Somerset and parts of Wiltshire and Gloucestershire.

The area has a varied and attractive landscape, wrinkled up into ridges which run roughly north-west to south-east. On the west coast, the ground drops dramatically from Exmoor towards Porlock and Minehead, then undulates through the heavily wooded Quantock Hills down to the absolutely flat Somerset Levels. North of Bristol, the land flattens out into the Vale of Berkeley where the Bristol Channel funnels between flat low banks into the River Severn. In the Cotswolds, to the north-east, the landscape begins to rise as limestone once more. In the south, the little valleys wind towards the rivers Frome and Axe. The hills rise as one gets closer to the sea to the south, with the Purbecks forming a narrow wave-like barrier, broken in the centre and guarded by the imposing ruins of Corfe Castle. This area has some of the most interesting and beautiful coastal scenery in Britain, as successive bands of clay and rock meet the sea and resist or erode, producing cliffs and landslips, little coves and stacks, and the long slender ribbon of Chesil Beach reaching out to the Isle of Portland. Much of this coast and the farming hinterland is owned by the National Trust.

The inhabitants of the coast are kept well aware of the sea by the mist and sudden squally winter gales, which bring a mingled, pleasing scent of sea air and heath. Inevitably, the west coast catches plenty of rain, but the climate is generally mild, and noticeably milder since the 1990s, according to tenants of the Golden Cap estate. This produces lush grazing and dairy produce, especially in Somerset, where the Levels resemble green baize in summer (see previous pages 34–35 for recipes using dairy produce from Wessex). The area is the traditional northern limit of the clotted cream tradition and cheese-making becomes the primary dairy activity. This has been important in Somerset since the 17th century, when Cheddar cheese was renowned for its excellence and size. The best farm-produced Somerset Cheddars have infinitely more character than blocks made by creameries, even those in the south-west. In the Gloucester area, milk from local Gloucester cattle, now a rare breed, helped the development of Gloucester cheese, double and single. Other cheeses are also produced in the area, including Caerphilly, which has been made in Somerset since the 19th century, Bath cheese, a soft square cheese, and the products of new-wave cheese-makers who have developed their own ideas, often using sheeps' or goats' milk.

The hillier land supports cattle and sheep for meat including local breeds such as North Devon cattle and Dorset sheep. Numerous other breeds are kept, including the rare Portland sheep, a 'primitive' or unimproved breed which is light and small. Pigs are also important (although the bacon industry around Calne in Wiltshire was founded in part on imported Irish pigs) but home-curing of bacon and ham is largely a thing of the past, partly because of regulations relating to killing and handling meat. Some butchers can still be relied on to stock Bath chaps (cooked pig's cheek), hog's puddings and chitterlings, and many local bakers make delicious, sticky lardy cakes.

The soft climate of Somerset and Gloucestershire is good for orchard fruit. Apples are grown for eating, cooking and cider-making. Interest in this drink has revived recently, and several makers produce versions made from single-variety apple juices. Cider is sometimes used in cakes, and apple cakes rely on chopped apple for their moisture. Other baking traditional to the area includes the rich Bath specialities of Bath buns and Sally Lunn bread.

The Aberdeen Angus cattle herd at Hindon Farm on Exmoor, Somerset.

A Dish of Cheese

This is really an Edwardian recipe for a savoury – a rich, highly flavoured little something served right at the end of a meal. Use a really good-quality Cheddar cheese for this Wessex recipe.

Put all the ingredients in a saucepan and heat gently, stirring continuously, until the mixture just comes to the boil. Serve in individual shallow dishes with rounds of toast for dipping and a salad of bitter leaves.

SERVES 4–6
AS A LIGHT LUNCH DISH

250g (9oz) Cheddar cheese, sliced
60ml (2fl oz) milk
150ml (¼ pint) single cream
2 whole eggs and 1 egg yolk
freshly ground black pepper

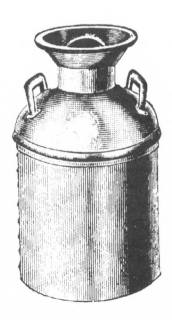

A Shropshire Breakfast

This recipe was recorded in the 1930s by Mrs Arthur Webb. It is an unusual and extremely good variation of cheese on toast from the Welsh Marches.

Fry the bacon. When cooked, put to the side and fry the bread in the bacon fat. Remove, cover with the sliced cheese and put under the grill to cook gently. Add the apple slices to the remaining bacon fat and fry gently, turning once or twice. When the cheese has melted, divide the bacon between the toasts and top with the apple slices. Dust the apple with a suspicion of sugar and grind a little pepper over everything.

For a lower-fat version, grill the bacon and toast the bread.

SERVES 4

4–8 rashers bacon (depending on
   size of rashers and appetites)
4 slices white bread
150g (5oz) Cheshire cheese,
   sliced
2 apples peeled, cored and sliced
a little sugar
pepper

Asparagus Tartlets

Asparagus is grown all over the country, but the Vale of Evesham in Worcestershire was famous for this crop.

Wash and trim the asparagus stems, cutting off the hard ends of the stalks. Place the asparagus in a pan and just cover with boiling water. Simmer until the stems are tender. Drain and cut the tips off and reserve. Put the rest in a processor or blender and reduce to a purée. Beat in the butter and season with salt and pepper. Stir in the egg yolks.

Roll out the pastry thinly and use to line patty tins. Divide the asparagus mixture between them. Decorate with the reserved tips and dot with butter.

Bake at 190°C, 375°F, Gas mark 5 for about 15 minutes. Serve warm.

MAKES 18

500g (1lb 2oz) asparagus
30g (1oz) butter, plus a
   little extra
salt and pepper
2 egg yolks
1 quantity shortcrust pastry
   (see page 13)

Tomato Tartlets

This was devised both to show off the best of West Country produce and make an interesting vegetarian dish, but it works so well that non-vegetarians will want some too.

To make the pastry, combine the Cheddar, clotted cream and flour, plus a little salt. Add just enough water to make the mixture into a dough, pressing it together with your fingers. Divide into 6, roll each piece into a circle and use to line the tins. Put the tins in the fridge for 30 minutes to rest the pastry.

For the filling, skin the tomatoes, quarter them and discard the seeds and pulp. Slice the flesh neatly. Smear a little of the mustard over the base of each pastry shell. Divide the tomatoes between them, sprinkling in the basil and parsley. Divide the Cheddar between the tartlets, and top each with a little knob of butter.

Bake at 220°C, 425°F, Gas mark 7 for 10–12 minutes. Best eaten warm.

MAKES 6

FOR THE PASTRY
80g (3oz) well-flavoured
   Cheddar, grated
80g (3oz) clotted cream
80g (3oz) plain flour
pinch of salt
4–5 teaspoons water

FOR THE FILLING
300–400g (10–14oz) tomatoes,
   preferably a firm-fleshed type
   (beef tomatoes, if nothing
   else is available)
2 teaspoons English mustard
1 tablespoon torn fresh basil
1 tablespoon chopped fresh
   parsley
40g (1½oz) Cheddar, grated
butter

You will need 6 tartlet tins,
9–10cm (3½–4in) in diameter

Little Cheese Tartlets

A variation on the theme of cheese baked with breadcrumbs, quite common in British cookery. This recipe comes from the borders of England and Scotland.

Grease a mince pie tray or patty tins well. Roll out the pastry thinly and use to line the patty tins. Grate the cheese finely, melt the butter and beat the eggs well. Add the cheese, butter, breadcrumbs and cream to the eggs, season with salt, pepper and cayenne, and divide between the pastry cases.

Bake at 220°C, 425°F, Gas mark 7 for 10–15 minutes. Serve warm.

MAKES 24

30g (1oz) butter, plus extra for greasing
1 quantity shortcrust pastry made with butter and lard mixed (see page 13)
200g (7oz) good Cheshire cheese
2 eggs
50g (1¾oz) fine white breadcrumbs
150ml (¼ pint) double cream
pepper and a pinch of salt
pinch of cayenne pepper

Leek Pasty

Leek puddings and pasties are a Northumbrian tradition. Try cheese in place of the bacon for a vegetarian version.

Plunge the leeks into boiling water for a minute, then drain them in a sieve. Press a plate over the top to remove as much liquid as possible, and leave to drain while you prepare the pie.

Roll out two-thirds of the pastry thinly and use to line a Swiss roll tin. Scatter the ham or bacon over the base. Put the drained leeks on top. Beat the eggs with the milk or cream and some pepper and pour over. Roll the rest of the pastry thinly, cover the pie and seal, crimping the edges with a fork. Brush over with beaten egg or milk. Bake at 200°C, 400°F, Gas mark 6 for 20 minutes.

SERVES 6
AS A LIGHT LUNCH OR SUPPER

500g (1lb 2oz) leeks, trimmed, washed and sliced
1 quantity shortcrust pastry made with butter and lard mixed (see page 13)
200g (7oz) lean bacon or ham, cut in small pieces
2 eggs
150ml (¼ pint) milk or thin cream
pepper
egg or milk, to glaze

You will need a Swiss roll tin

Little Cheese Puddings

These puddings are a bit like a baked Welsh rarebit, adapted from a much heftier Welsh recipe given by Bobby Freeman.

Toast the bread on one side under the grill. Butter the untoasted side. Line each ramekin with a slice, toasted side down. Divide the cheese between the dishes. Bring the cream to the boil, add the seasonings and spices and beat in the eggs. Pour over the bread and cheese. Rest for 30 minutes, then bake at 190°C, 375°F, Gas mark 5 for 20–25 minutes, until well-risen and light brown. Serve immediately with a salad of watercress or bitter leaves.

SERVES 6
AS A LIGHT LUNCH

6 thin slices white bread,
   crusts removed
butter, for spreading and greasing
120g (4oz) Cheddar, grated
180ml (6fl oz) single cream
½ teaspoon dry mustard
pepper
pinch of cayenne
nutmeg
5 eggs, beaten

You will need 6 individual
ovenproof ramekins, buttered

Welsh Rarebit

There are at least three basic versions of this toasted cheese dish. This is one of the more elaborate versions.

Put everything except the bread in a pan. Stir well and heat gently until all is melted and well amalgamated. Spread over the untoasted side of the bread and brown under the grill.

SERVES 4

200g (7oz) strong cheese,
    such as Cheddar or a good
    Cheshire, grated
30g (1oz) butter
1 teaspoon dry mustard powder
2 teaspoons plain flour
4 tablespoons beer
pepper
4 slices bread, toasted on one side

Potted Beef

A survival from the 18th-century tradition of making meat or fish into pastes to preserve under a layer of clarified butter. In Yorkshire it often appeared as a sandwich filling at festive teas.

Put the beef in an ovenproof dish and add water up to the level of the top of the meat. Stew gently with the bay leaf for about 3 hours in a low oven 150°C, 300°F, Gas mark 2 until very tender. When well done, drain off the gravy and reserve.

Take out the bay leaf and shred the meat, removing any very obvious bits of fat or gristle. Add the salt, mace, black pepper, vinegar and butter. Either put the mixture through a processor briefly, but don't overdo it. Add some of the reserved gravy: the mixture should be moist but not sloppy.

Pack into 2 ramekins. Clarify the remaining butter by heating it in a small pan until it foams. Allow it to stand so that the sediment can settle at the bottom of the pan, then skim off and discard the foam and gently pour the liquid butter over the top of the meat to seal. Store in the fridge and use within a few days.

SERVES 2

250g (9oz) stewing beef, cut
   into small pieces
1 bay leaf
½ teaspoon salt
½ teaspoon ground mace
generous grind of black pepper
2 tablespoons sherry vinegar
60g (2oz) butter, plus at least
   60g (2oz) for the top of the pot

Ham Loaf

One 19th-century wit defined eternity as 'two people and a ham'. This recipe is one way to use the remains of a large piece when boredom has set in.

Mince the ham or put it through a food processor until finely chopped. Bring the milk to the boil and soak the bread in it. Mix with the ham, grinding in some black pepper and adding the mace, cloves and parsley. Taste and add a little salt if the mixture seems bland. Beat in the egg to bind.

Grease the inside of the terrine or loaf tin with butter and pack the mixture into it. Cover with buttered paper or foil. Bake at 180°C, 350°F, Gas mark 4 for 1 hour. Allow to cool, chill and turn out. Serve with salad.

500g (1lb 2oz) cooked ham, a quarter of which should be fat
125ml (4fl oz) milk
60g (2oz) crustless white bread
black pepper
½ teaspoon ground mace
¼ teaspoon ground cloves
2 tablespoons finely chopped fresh parsley
1 egg
butter for greasing

You will need a terrine or loaf tin

Jellied Beef in Brown Ale

Much of the land owned by the National Trust is in areas of hilly landscapes, especially in the north and west of the country. Such land is best suited to grazing cattle and sheep, and in consequence, the farms produce much beef and lamb (and sometimes mutton). Many of the dishes in this book were devised to make good use of this meat. This recipe and the one on page 76 were originally made with produce from farms owned by the National Trust in Northumberland, where some of the animals graze alongside Hadrian's Wall as it traces a line across the countryside past Housesteads Fort.

They were also intended to use less glamorous cuts of meat in response to a complaint I heard several times from farmers' wives involved in marketing projects in several parts of the country: that everyone wanted steaks, chops and prime cuts such as sirloin of beef or leg of lamb. Knowing how to make good use of all cuts was of great importance in farmhouses where money and time were both tight. One response was to leave food to cook in a low oven all morning, which works well with secondary cuts such as brisket of beef – a well-flavoured piece of meat, but one best cooked long and slow.

SERVES 8–10

dripping or oil
1.5–2kg (3¼–4½lb) beef brisket, boned and rolled
300ml (½ pint) brown ale
1 pig's trotter
1½ teaspoons salt
bouquet garni of bay leaf, parsley and thyme
1 garlic clove, bruised

You will need a pot in which the meat fits neatly

Melt the dripping or oil and brown the meat all round. Add the brown ale and let it bubble. Put in the trotter and add the salt, herbs and garlic. Finally, add cold water to about three-quarters of the way up the meat. Bring to the boil, cover with tinfoil and the lid of the pot. Simmer very gently for 3 hours, or cook in a low oven at 170°C, 325°F, Gas mark 3. It doesn't matter if it cooks a bit longer.

Allow the whole thing to cool, then lift the beef onto a plate, cover and cool completely. Bring the cooking liquor back to the boil and reduce by a third. Strain into a basin and chill. Lift off any fat which has risen to the surface. The stock underneath should have set to a firm brown jelly.

To serve, slice the beef neatly and arrange on a long dish. Chop the jelly and arrange down either side of the meat. Serve with salad and potatoes for a summer meal.

Valerie Burke's Orchard Picnic Loaf

Sometimes there just isn't enough time to do everything, which is how Mrs Burke made the sausage-roll filling into a meatloaf one day. The fruit included is in celebration of the orchard at her farm in Pembrokeshire.

Beat the eggs in a large mixing bowl. Stir in all the herbs and seasonings. Add the sausage meat and mix well with a fork or clean hands. Stir in the onion, apple and pear.

Place the mixture in the loaf tin and bake at 190°C, 375°F, Gas mark 5 for 50–60 minutes. Cool, turn out onto a dish, slice and serve with a watercress salad.

2 eggs
1 tablespoon chopped fresh herbs
salt and pepper
1 teaspoon English mustard
750g (1lb 10oz) good-quality pork
    sausage meat
1 onion, finely chopped
1 cooking apple, chopped
1 pear, chopped

You will need a 900g (2lb) loaf tin, lightly greased

Ham Cooked in Cider

I tested this recipe using mild, succulent gammon from Hindon Farm. The farm produce has won several awards for excellence. The ham is cured in traditional Devon fashion, although Hindon, on the Holnicote Estate, is actually just over the Somerset border. The recipe was originally given by Theodora Fitzgibbon in the 1970s.

Soak the ham overnight in cold water. Drain, put into a pan in which it fits snugly and add all the other ingredients except the breadcrumbs. Bring to the boil, turn the heat down to simmer and cook for 25 minutes per 500g (1lb 2oz). Leave in the stock until almost cold, then remove and allow to drain (keep the stock, providing it is not too salty, as it makes a very good soup).

To serve, remove the skin of the ham with a sharp knife and press the browned breadcrumbs on to the fat.

SERVES 10–12

2.5kg (5½lb) Devon-cured ham in a piece

1–1.5 litre (1¾–2½ pints) dry cider

1 large onion, peeled and stuck with 6–8 cloves

1 tablespoon brown sugar

1 lemon

2–3 sprigs fresh parsley and marjoram

a few peppercorns

3 tablespoons browned breadcrumbs for coating the meat

Pork Pie

In the past, pork pies showed local variations in recipe and method and a good pie was a source of pride to a housewife or local butcher. Skilled pie-makers raised the crust entirely by hand, giving it a slightly baggy appearance, or shaped the pastry over a cylindrical form which was removed to leave space for the filling. Using a cake tin gives more certain results, even if the pie loses a hand-made appearance.

Melton Mowbray in Leicestershire still produces a distinctive pie, and this recipe incorporates elements of that tradition – anchovy essence as a flavouring, and fresh meat instead of brined. The pastry recipe, from Derbyshire, is unusual in the combination of fats. Lard is the usual choice, and can be used for the total weight of fat in this recipe if desired. The method for the jellied stock was worked out by Jane Grigson as a better alternative to gelatine-fortified stock now used by many pie-makers. The stock can be made in advance, but the pastry should be as fresh as possible.

Place the stock ingredients in a large pan and bring to the boil. Skim well and simmer, covered, for about 3 hours. Strain the liquid into a clean pan and discard the debris. Boil the stock to reduce it to around 500ml (18fl oz). Leave to cool and jellify. Refrigerate until needed.

Cut a quarter of the leanest pork into cubes 1cm (½in) across. Mince the rest coarsely – this is best done by hand with a sharp knife, as a mincer tends to compact the meat. Add the seasonings and turn well so they are evenly distributed through the meat.

MAKES 1 LARGE PIE,
WHICH WILL SERVE 10

FOR THE STOCK
2 pig's trotters
bones, skin or trimmings
    from the pie meat
1 bay leaf
2–3 sprigs thyme
4 peppercorns
1 onion, stuck with cloves
3 litres (5¼ pints) water

FOR THE FILLING
1kg (2¼lb) pork, a quarter of
    which should be fatty, the rest
    lean; I use a mixture of
    shoulder and belly
1 teaspoon salt
1 teaspoon anchovy essence
pepper
6–8 sage leaves, chopped

For the pastry, put the flour in a large bowl and add the salt. Measure the water into a pan and add the fats. Heat the pan, stirring, until the water has come to the boil and all the fat has melted. Remove the pan from the heat and stir the mixture into the flour. Use a wooden spoon at first, then, as it cools slightly, knead to make sure it is all incorporated properly. Cover the bowl and keep it in a warm place.

To raise the pie, take three-quarters of the pastry, still warm, and shape it into a disc. Put it in the cake tin and quickly raise it up the sides to the top, making it as even as possible and trying not to get the pastry too thick. The dough should be malleable – if it flops, it is too warm. Once the pastry is raised, pack the filling into it. Roll out the remaining quarter to make a lid and brush the edges with beaten egg. Trim any excess and crimp the edges. Make a small hole in the middle and cover it with a pastry rose. Cut leaves from the trimmings and use them to decorate the top of the pie. Brush with beaten egg.

Bake at 200°C, 400°F, Gas mark 6 for 30 minutes, then lower the heat to 170°C, 325°F, Gas mark 3 and bake for another 1½ hours. Some gravy may bubble out of the pie, but don't worry too much about this – some recipes cite this as an indication that the pie is cooked.

At the end of cooking time, remove the pie from the oven and allow to stand for 20 minutes. Take the jellied stock, and if it has cooled off, reheat to boiling. Ease off the pastry rose and pour in as much hot stock as the pie will hold. Replace the rose and allow the pie to cool. Wait 24 hours before cutting.

FOR THE PASTRY
450g (1lb) plain flour
½ teaspoon salt
150ml (¼ pint) water
60g (2oz) lard
60g (2oz) butter
30g (1oz) suet
1 egg, beaten, to seal and glaze

You will need an 18–19cm (7–7½in) round, sprung cake tin with a removable base

Game Pie

Game pie, historically, would be made only on wealthy farms with large amounts of land over which the men could shoot as in East Anglia. It can be made in the same way as pork pie (see page 54) with hot-water crust and jellied stock, using 450g (1lb) meat from game and the same from pork. This version is a bit of a hybrid between a raised pie and a more standard short pastry version, devised when I had a lot of leftover game to deal with.

Line the base of the cake tin with greaseproof paper. Make the sauce for the filling first. Melt the butter in a large frying pan. Brown the cubed venison, the sausage meat and the other game if it is raw. Remove, leaving as much fat as possible in the pan. Stir in the flour. Add the wine, scraping the bottom of the pan to pick up all the residues from the game. Pour in the stock and simmer gently for about 20 minutes. Taste, and add salt, pepper and a scrape of nutmeg. The sauce should be well seasoned. Turn into a basin and allow to cool to tepid.

SERVES 10 EASILY

FOR THE FILLING
50g (1¾oz) butter
450g (1lb) venison, diced
400–500g (14oz–1lb 2oz) good pork sausage meat, divided into 10–12 balls
450g (1lb) assorted other game, cut off the bone (for example, pheasant, pigeon, partridge, rabbit, hare; cooked game can be used)
2 tablespoons flour
100ml (3½fl oz) red wine
300ml (½ pint) stock, made from the bones and trimmings of game birds cooked with an onion and 1 bouquet garni
salt and pepper
nutmeg

Roll three-quarters of the pastry into a large circle and place in the tin, so that it drapes over the sides. Ease it down onto the base, into the edges and up the sides, trying not to stretch it. You will have to make small pleats in places. Roll out the remaining quarter for the lid. Distribute the venison evenly over the base and top with the other game, arranging it so that each portion will get a share of something nice. Add the sausage meat balls. Pour in the sauce. Cover with the pastry lid, sealing with beaten egg. Trim, crimp the edges decoratively and add decorations of pastry flowers and leaves. Game pies should be very ornamental. Glaze with beaten egg.

Place on a heated baking tray in a hot oven, 220°C, 425°F, Gas mark 7 for 20–30 minutes (watch to see it doesn't brown too quickly), then turn the temperature down to 170°C, 325°F, Gas mark 3 and cook for a further 1½ hours. Remove the pie from the oven. Allow to cool in the tin overnight and serve cold.

FOR THE PASTRY
shortcrust pastry (see page 13
 for the method) made from:
450g (1lb) plain flour
100g (3½oz) butter
120g (4oz) lard
1 teaspoon salt
100ml (3½fl oz) water
1 egg, beaten, to seal and glaze

You will need a circular cake
tin 20–23cm (8–9in) round
cake tin, preferably with a loose
bottom. Don't use a tin with an
insulated base, or the pastry
won't cook properly.

Cornish Pasties

Pasties – or oggies – are made all over Cornwall but the quality varies, to put it politely. Made with fresh ingredients and good meat, they are a fine thing.

Make the pastry. Let it rest for about 30 minutes, then roll out to 5mm (⅕in) thick and cut two dinner plate-sized rounds. Mix the vegetables and use to cover half of each piece of pastry. Season the meat well and cover the vegetables. Wet the edges of the pastry, fold over and crimp the edges; brush with milk or beaten egg to glaze. Bake on a lightly greased tray, starting in a hot oven 200°C, 400°F, Gas mark 6. After 15 minutes, lower the heat to 180°C, 350°F, Gas mark 4 and cook for another 45 minutes.

MAKES 2 LARGE PASTIES

1 quantity shortcrust pastry (see page 13)
200g (7oz) potato, peeled and chopped
100g (3½oz) raw turnip, chopped
60g (2oz) onion, chopped
250–300g (9–10oz) steak chuck or skirt, finely chopped (don't use minced beef)
salt and pepper
milk or beaten egg to glaze

Bacon and Spinach Pie

This pie is a recipe from the south-west and another example of the Cornish habit of enclosing everything in pastry.

Trim the bacon of any excess fat and use a little of this to soften the chopped shallot in a frying pan. Blanch the spinach by plunging it into boiling water and draining well – put it in a sieve and press to remove excess water.

Use a third of the bacon to line the base of a pie dish. Cover with half the chopped spinach, scatter half the watercress and parsley over, then add the softened shallots. Cover with another third of the bacon, then add the rest of the greenery. Beat the eggs with the cream and a little pepper but no salt (the bacon will probably provide enough), and pour over. Top with the rest of the bacon. Roll out the pastry, cover the dish and crimp the edges. Bake at 170°C, 325°F, Gas mark 3 for 1 hour. Serve hot.

SERVES 4

250g (9oz) rashers bacon
3–4 shallots, finely chopped
250g (9oz) spinach
1 bunch of watercress, chopped
1 handful of parsley, chopped
2 eggs, beaten
60ml (2fl oz) single cream
pepper
1 quantity shortcrust pastry made
   with butter and lard mixed (see
   page 13)

Cheddar Pork Pie

A Somerset recipe, collected in the area around the village of Cheddar by Mrs Arthur Webb. It is a pie in the sense that shepherd's pie is – the covering is potato, not pastry.

Mix the flour with the salt and some pepper and toss the pork in it. Smear the inside of an ovenproof casserole with a little dripping and put in the pork. Add the stock and apple brandy. Cover with a layer of apple rings, then onion, then potatoes; season these with a little salt and pepper and the sage. Then repeat, ending in a layer of potato. Grease a piece of foil with dripping and cover tightly. Cook at 170°C, 325°F, Gas mark 3 for 2 hours.

Uncover 30 minutes before the end of cooking, and turn the heat up to 190°C, 375°F, Gas mark 5 to crisp and brown the potatoes.

SERVES 4

2 tablespoons plain flour

½ teaspoon salt and some pepper

500g (1lb 2oz) lean pork, diced in 1cm (½in) cubes

dripping or oil

150ml (¼ pint) stock or water

2 tablespoons apple brandy (if this isn't available, whisky is the best substitute)

2–3 sweet apples, peeled, cored and sliced in rings

1 very large or 2 medium onions, sliced

4–5 large potatoes, peeled and thickly sliced

5–6 sage leaves, chopped

Smothered Chicken

A re-working of an old Dorset recipe for cooking rabbits.

Flour the chicken and pack into the dish. Add cider until it half covers the chicken. Lay the bacon rashers over. Mix the breadcrumbs, onions, thyme and lemon zest and season with a little salt and pepper. Add just enough egg to bind the mixture lightly (don't make it wet or try to press it together). Spoon over the meat.

Bake gently at 170–180°C, 325–350°F, Gas mark 3–4 for 1½ hours – a little longer won't harm it. Towards the end of cooking, look to see if the cider is drying out, and add a little more if necessary.

SERVES 4–6

plain flour, for dusting
4 chicken joints, skinned, the legs divided into thighs and drumsticks, breasts cut in two
4–6 rashers lean bacon
250ml (9fl oz) dry cider
200g (7oz) fine white breadcrumbs
2 medium onions, finely chopped
1 teaspoon chopped fresh thyme
1 teaspoon grated lemon zest
salt and pepper
1 egg, beaten for binding

You will need an ovenproof dish that holds the chicken neatly in one layer

Potato Case Pie

A recipe from Suffolk, recorded in the 1930s. Similar to shepherd's pie, it is simple and good.

Boil the potatoes until soft. Drain and mash with the butter; season with salt and pepper and work in the flour.

Mix the ham and onion and season with pepper, a scrape of nutmeg, the leaves picked from the thyme and the parsley. Stir well and add a couple of tablespoons water, or a little stock or gravy if you have it.

Generously butter the cake tin. Take two-thirds of the potato mixture and spread it evenly over the base and about 2.5cm (1in) up the sides. Spread the seasoned ham over the potato. Use the remaining potato mixture to cover the ham, pressing the two layers together at the sides. Use the tines of a fork to make a nice pattern on top. Bake at 220°C, 425°F, Gas mark 7 for 30 minutes, by which time the edges and top will be deliciously brown.

SERVES 3–4
AS A LIGHT MEAL

500g (1lb 2oz) floury potatoes, peeled and cut into chunks
30g (1oz) butter, plus a little extra for greasing
salt and pepper
50g (1¾oz) plain flour
120g (4oz) ham, trimmed of any fat and minced
½ small onion, finely chopped
nutmeg
3–4 sprigs thyme
heaped teaspoon chopped fresh parsley

You will need an 18–20cm (7–8in) round cake tin with a loose bottom

Forfar Bridies

Named after the town of Forfar, just north of Dundee, a bridie is similar in concept to a Cornish pasty.

Make the pastry first. The fat must be cold from the fridge. Put the flour and salt in a bowl. Using the coarse side of a grater, grate the butter and lard into the flour (periodically dipping the fat into the flour makes this easier). Once all the fat is in, start adding iced water, a tablespoon at a time, stirring the mixture with your hands until a stiff paste forms. Don't overdo the water: the mixture needs to be coherent but not sticky. Turn it onto a floured work surface and work for a moment, just enough to make sure the mixture is even. Then roll out into an oblong three times as long as it is wide; turn the top third down towards you and the bottom third up to cover this. Turn 90 degrees clockwise and repeat the rolling and folding process, then chill for 30 minutes. Repeat this rolling and folding process twice more, give the pastry a final 30-minute rest and it is ready for use. It can be made a day in advance; if you do this, wrap it in foil or clingfilm and store in the fridge overnight.

To prepare the filling, trim all fat and gristle from the meat. Cut it in slices about 5mm (¼in) thick, and then into strips. Cut across to make tiny dice. Season with 1 teaspoon salt and a generous sprinkle of black pepper and mixed well.

Divide the pastry into three and roll each piece out to an oval about 5mm (¼in) thick. Put one-third of the meat on each oval. Divide the suet, and the onion if using, between the bridies, scattering over the meat. Wet the edges of the pastry and seal, crimping the edges (the seam should run down one side). Cut a small hole in the top of each one.

Put them on a baking sheet and cook in a hot oven, 220°C, 425°F, Gas mark 7 for 20 minutes, then reduce to 170°C, 325°F, Gas mark 3 and cook for about 1 hour.

MAKES 3 BRIDIES

FOR THE PASTRY
250g (9oz) flour, plus extra
    for working and rolling
½ teaspoon salt
175g (6oz) fat (equal quantities
    of butter and lard), chilled
iced water

FOR THE FILLING
500g (about 1lb) steak
    ('best steak' is usually
    quoted – rump steak is fine,
    if the housekeeping runs to it,
    but a good quality braising
    steak will work)
salt and pepper
about 30g (1oz) suet
1 small onion, finely chopped
    (optional)

Grouse Pie

Huge areas of the Scottish highlands are dominated by a patchwork of heather moorland, managed by rotational burning of small patches to provide food and cover for grouse.

Roast the birds in a hot oven, 220°C, 425°F, Gas mark 7 for 15 minutes. Allow to cool. Skin, carve the meat off neatly and divide into 8 or 10 pieces per bird – cut the legs through at the joints, slice through the breasts close to the wings, and cut the breasts in half. Arrange neatly in a pie dish.

Take the grouse skin, trimmings and bones (break them up) and put in a pan with the ham and sherry. Heat until the wine bubbles, then add the onion, herbs and allspice. Pour over the stock and top up with water to cover the solids. Cover and cook gently for an hour. Strain, discarding the debris; you should have about 450ml (¾ pint) of stock (if not, return it to a clean saucepan and reduce).

Melt the butter in a saucepan and stir in the flour to make a roux. Allow it to cook gently and brown a little. Incorporate the stock bit by bit to make a smooth sauce. Add a little redcurrant jelly, season and taste; you may not want to use all the jelly. Pour over the meat and allow to cool.

When ready to cook the pie, dust a work surface with flour and roll out the pastry to about 5mm (¼in) thick. Cut a strip about 2cm (¾in) wide. Wet the edge of the pie dish and lay the pastry around it. Then trim the rest to make the lid and lay over the filling. Crimp the edges and use the trimmings to make a rose for the centre and decorative leaves for the top of the pie. Brush with beaten egg, milk or cream.

Bake at 200°C, 400°F, Gas mark 6 for 20 minutes, then reduce the heat to 180°C, 350°F, Gas mark 4 and cook for a further 10–20 minutes until the meat is cooked through and the gravy bubbling.

SERVES 4

a brace of grouse
a slice of ham or some trimmings
    from a ham joint
about 100ml (3½fl oz)
    medium sherry
½ onion, sliced
2 bay leaves
a few sprigs fresh parsley
    and thyme
3–4 whole allspice berries
30g (1oz) butter
30g (1oz) plain flour, plus
    extra for dusting
about a dessertspoon
    redcurrant jelly
salt and pepper
puff pastry
beaten egg, milk or cream to
    brush over the top of the pie

Bill's Burgers

There is a lot of very good lamb and beef production on National Trust land in the Salcombe area of Devon. Photographer Bill Butt put his burger recipe on the Well Hung Meat Company website (www.wellhungmeat.com), and all parties have kindly allowed me to quote it.

Finely chop the shallots, garlic, coriander and thyme. Mix them with the mince. Stir in the salt. Scrunch together in balls of around 200g (7oz) before flattening them into burgers. A little egg and breadcrumbs can help bind the burgers but this is not essential. Place the burgers under a hot grill or on a griddle and cook to your preference.

MAKES 5–6 BURGERS

100g (3½oz) shallots
2–3 garlic cloves
handful of fresh coriander
handful of fresh thyme (strip
    out the woodiest stalks)
1kg (2¼lb) lean minced beef
1 teaspoon salt
1 egg, beaten, and breadcrumbs
    for binding (optional)

Saucer Pies

As one travels further north towards the Scottish Borders, pie fillings depend less on pork products and more on beef, or mutton, like these little pies. The mutton or lamb can be cooked or raw, but give the latter a longer initial cooking time.

Melt the dripping and fry the shallots and garlic gently for a few minutes. Add the meat and mushrooms and cook over a moderate heat until browned. Stir in the stock, herbs and a little seasoning. Stew gently, giving pre-cooked meat 10 minutes, raw meat about 40 minutes. If you have some good gravy left over from a roast, add this at the end and allow it to bubble for a few minutes. Taste and correct the seasoning. Leave to cool.

Divide the pastry into 8 and roll each piece into a circle as big as a saucer. Press 4 pieces into saucers and divide the filling between them. Top with the reserved pastry circles, seal, trim and crimp the edges with the tines of a fork. Brush over with glaze. Bake at 220°C, 425°F, Gas mark 7 for 20–25 minutes.

MAKES 4 LITTLE PIES

beef dripping
2 shallots, chopped
1 garlic clove, crushed
300–350g (10oz–12oz) cooked neck of lamb or mutton, trimmed of fat and chopped fairly finely
120–150g (4–5oz) mushrooms, sliced
3–4 tablespoons of stock made from the bones of the lamb
2–3 tablespoons chopped fresh parsley
2–3 sprigs chopped fresh thyme
salt and pepper
a little gravy from lamb or beef (not essential, but a good addition)
1 quantity shortcrust pastry made with lard (see page 13)
milk or beaten egg to glaze

Cornish Fish Pie

Cornish farmhouse traditions mix fish and dairy produce. The fresh wild sea bass used in this recipe is in season between August and March; smaller farmed fish are available all year round. Ask your fishmonger for some bones and trimmings for stock.

Put the fish bones and trimmings in a small pan, cover with water and simmer gently for 20 minutes to produce a little fish stock. Cut the fish fillets into slices about 3cm (1¼in) wide. Grease the pie dish and lay the fish in it. Scatter salt, pepper and chopped parsley over. Add 4 tablespoons of the fish stock.

Roll out the pastry and top the pie with it, trimming neatly. Cut a hole in the centre and make a pastry rose to cover it. Bake the pie for about 15 minutes at 220°C, 425°F, Gas mark 7. Warm the single cream gently until almost boiling. Lift the pastry rose and pour the warmed cream into the pie. Return to the oven for another 5 minutes. Just before serving, lift the crust at the edge and place the clotted cream over the fish.

SERVES 4

450g (1lb) sea bass fillets, skinned; use the bones and trimmings to make a little stock
a little butter for greasing
salt and pepper
1 tablespoon chopped fresh parsley
1 quantity shortcrust pastry made with butter and lard mixed (see page 13)
100ml (3½fl oz) single cream
2 tablespoons clotted cream

Choose a pie dish that will hold the fish neatly

Oatmeal Herring and Nettle Champ

I am indebted to Fionnuala Jay-O'Boyle at Taste of Ulster for this Irish recipe. Her grandmother used to make this for tea. It is well worth trying, a delicious combination of textures and flavours.

Mix the salt with the oatmeal and coat the herrings with it. Melt the butter in a frying pan and fry the fish over a low heat. Whole herrings will need about 5 minutes per side, fillets will take 3 minutes per side. The skin should be beautifully brown and crisp.

Serve with nettle champ. Following the recipe on page 148, substitute two handfuls of young nettles for the chives or spring onions (use rubber gloves when you gather nettles). Wash, blanch and coarsely chop before adding to the dish.

SERVES 2

½ teaspoon salt
15g (½oz) fine oatmeal
2 fresh herrings, cleaned, but with the heads on (use filleted herring if you prefer)
30g (1oz) butter for frying

Smoked Haddock and New Potato Salad

Fish smoking was particularly associated with the Scottish coast from Fife northwards to Aberdeen. If you can buy the little smoked haddock known as Arbroath smokies, they are good in this dish, and need no preliminary cooking, as the process uses hot smoke which cooks the fish.

The ingredients for this salad recall those for Cullen skink, a chowder-like soup of smoked haddock and potatoes and a Scottish speciality (Cullen is in Moray, on the north-east coast of Scotland).

If using cold-smoked haddock, put the fish in a shallow ovenproof dish and cover with the milk. Cook at 190°C, 375°F, Gas mark 5 for 15–20 minutes until the fish is opaque and flakes away from the skin easily. Drain and allow to cool a little, then remove and discard all skin and flake the flesh. Take care to try and remove all bones as you do this. If using smokies, cooking is unnecessary, but the skin and bone will still have to be removed.

Cover the potatoes with water and cook until tender. Drain and cut into quarters if very small, or large cubes if bigger. Cut the spring onions obliquely in fine slices and mix with the potatoes while they are still warm.

Make a dressing using the lemon juice and olive oil, seasoning with salt and pepper. Toss the potatoes and spring onions in this, then mix in the fish. Garnish with chopped parsley and serve, just cooled.

SERVES 4 AS A LIGHT LUNCH
OR STARTER

about 300g (10oz) undyed smoked
    haddock or 2 Arbroath smokies
about 300ml (½ pint) milk (if
    using cold-smoked haddock)
about 400g (14oz) new potatoes
half a bunch of spring onions,
    washed and trimmed
1 tablespoon lemon juice
3 tablespoons olive oil
salt and pepper
chopped fresh parsley

Hearty Meals

Julia Horner's Cushion of Lamb

The Horner family have farmed at Redmire Farm, on the Upper Wharfedale estate in Yorkshire, for over 80 years. Like other farmers on the estate they breed sheep, which provide foundation stock for commercial lamb production. The local sheep are horned, black-faced, raggedy-fleeced Dalesbreds and Swaledales, hardy enough to spend most of their lives grazing the herb-rich limestone pastures and heather moorlands of the nearby 'tops'. Some are pure-bred to continue the bloodlines for next year's stock. Others are cross-bred with Leicester or Suffolk rams, to provide mothers for another generation of lambs further down the dale. Inevitably, some are surplus to requirements, which forced Julia Horner to think creatively about marketing her lamb. A local butcher taught her methods for cutting and boning the meat, and a small abattoir a few miles away in Wensleydale agreed to work to her specifications. She uses the Dalesbred lamb, small-boned and sweet, for direct marketing and lets the cross-breds go to market. Her Dalesbreds provide the basis for some imaginatively cut joints including the 'cushion', a trimmed, boned shoulder neatly tied in a little square, and seasoned with bay and juniper.

SERVES 4

beef dripping or oil
1 cushion (trimmed, boned
    and tied shoulder) of lamb
200g (7oz) each chopped onion,
    diced turnip, diced carrot and
    diced celery
salt and pepper
100ml (3½fl oz) stock or water
redcurrant jelly, to serve

You will need a casserole dish,
preferably a small cast-iron one,
in which the meat will fit neatly

Melt a little dripping or oil and brown the meat all over. Put the chopped vegetables in the bottom of the casserole and fit the meat on top. Add a little salt and pepper, and just enough water or stock to cover the bottom of the pot. Cover and transfer to a very low oven, 150–170°C, 300–325°F, Gas mark 2–3 for 3 hours.

Remove the meat to a warm dish and tip the rest of the contents into a sieve over a bowl. Strain into a pan, pressing the vegetables to extract the juices, then discard the vegetables left in the sieve. Skim off the fat and reduce the juices until syrupy by fast boiling. Check the seasoning.

Carve the meat in wedges as if cutting a melon, and serve with the sauce and freshly steamed vegetables. Serve some redcurrant jelly separately.

Hadrian's Wall Lamb with Root Vegetables

Hadrian's Wall snakes across Northumberland, for some of its route following a ridge of hard rock known as Whin Sill. National Trust farms here produce grass-fed lamb and beef – both new season and wether (grown on to 18 months old) – as Hadrian's Wall Lamb and Beef. This recipe can be used with a whole or half shoulder, or with neck of lamb, halved lengthways.

Put the oil and salt in a roasting tin. Turn all the vegetables and the garlic in the oil until well coated. Put the meat on top, tucking the rosemary and thyme underneath. Sprinkle the meat with a little salt. Cover with foil, sealing it round the sides of the tin. Cook at 230°C, 450°F, Gas mark 8 for 30 minutes, then turn the heat down to 140°C, 275°F, Gas mark 1 and leave it for 2½–3 hours.

Remove the lamb from the oven and turn the heat up to 220°C, 425°F, Gas mark 7. Put the meat on a warm plate and leave in a warm place. Discard the herbs. Pour as much of the fat and juice as possible from the roasting tin into a bowl, stir the vegetables around gently and then return them, in the tin, to the oven for 10 minutes to brown and crisp a little. Extract as much fat as possible from the juices. Chilling it briefly in the fridge solidifies the fat and makes it easier to remove but you will need to reheat the juices.

Serve the meat, which will be falling off the bone, vegetables and pan juices together, plus a little redcurrant jelly on the side.

SERVES 4

1 tablespoon oil
½ teaspoon salt
700g (1½lb) potatoes, peeled and cut into eighths
150g (5oz) turnips, peeled and cut into 1–2.5cm (½–1in) dice
150g (5oz) parsnips, peeled and cut in chunks
150g (5oz) carrots, peeled and cut in thick slices
1 head fresh garlic, cloves separated, peeled and left whole
1 small shoulder or two necks of lamb
4 sprigs fresh rosemary
8 sprigs fresh thyme
redcurrant jelly to serve

Slow-Roast Herdwick Mutton with Salsa Verde

Herdwick sheep have been grazing the Lake District fells for centuries and are now a rare breed, mostly confined to this area. They have a distinctive appearance, with pale heads, small curved horns and rusty brown or grey fleeces. Grazing sheep help to maintain the bare, grassy slopes of many of the hills but the importance of Herdwick sheep as a food source is reflected both in the lamb- or mutton-based 'tatie pot' (see page 81) and in special dishes made for busy days like at sheep-clipping time. Their survival owes much to Beatrix Potter, a sheep farmer as well as a children's writer, who left her land to the National Trust on condition that Herdwicks were grazed on it in perpetuity.

Several traditional Lake District recipes use their meat, but local butchers and farmers such as Hazel Relph at Yew Tree Farm and the Flock-In Tea Room in Borrowdale (www.borrowdaleherdwick.co.uk) have developed their own ideas for cooking it, including 'Herdi-burgers'.

SERVES 6

1 leg of lamb or mutton,
    2.5–3kg (5½–6½lb)
salt and pepper

FOR THE SALSA VERDE
a generous handful each of
    mint, parsley, basil
1 small garlic clove, crushed
2 tablespoons capers, rinsed
2 tablespoons Dijon mustard
2 tablespoons red wine vinegar
8 tablespoons olive oil
salt

The ingredients of salsa verde echo the English traditions of caper sauce with mutton and mint sauce with lamb. I first came across the idea of serving it with Herdwick mutton at a Heritage Feast cooked by Joy Davies and Gareth Jones for Slow Food.

If you're lucky enough to acquire a leg of Herdwick mutton, cook it very slowly at 140°C, 275°F, Gas mark 1, allowing 1 hour per 500g (1lb 2oz). Season with salt and pepper towards the end of cooking. Otherwise support your region's farming community and source some good-quality lamb from your local area and follow your preferred roasting method.

To make the salsa verde, wash the herbs and pick the leaves off, discarding the stalks. Blend all the ingredients together, taste and season.

Carve the meat in wedges, starting by cutting a slice halfway between the aitchbone (hip joint) and knuckle, then working outwards in each direction. Serve the salsa verde seperately.

Lamb Steaks with Quince

Mark and Charlotte Russell raise delicious lamb at Lanteglos, near Fowey in Cornwall. They sell some at their farm but to buy steaks you'll have to go to Devon, to the Riverford Farm Shop, Staverton, near Totnes (www.riverfordfarmshop.co.uk), where Ben Watson seams the leg meat into individual muscles. He suggested this way of cooking them.

Put a little olive oil in a small pan. Add the shallots and rosemary and cook slowly until soft. Drain off any excess oil and discard the rosemary.

Melt half the butter in a large frying pan. When hot, add the lamb steaks and fry rapidly on both sides until done to your taste. Remove to a heated plate and keep warm while you make the sauce. Add the remaining butter and the cooked shallots. Fry quickly, then add the garlic and cook a little longer, but don't let it brown. Add the stock, turn up the heat and cook rapidly until syrupy. Stir in the cream and let it amalgamate. Then add the quince jelly and cook, stirring for a few moments to mix thoroughly. Taste, correct the seasoning and add a squeeze of lemon juice if the quince jelly is on the bland side. Serve with the steaks.

SERVES 4

a little olive oil

8 shallots, sliced

1 sprig rosemary

30g (1oz) butter

4 lamb leg steaks, each weighing about 150–200g (5–7oz) – if you can't buy neat, lean steaks use neck fillet, cut in slices

4 garlic cloves, sliced

200ml (7fl oz) light chicken or beef stock

60ml (2fl oz) double cream

40g (1½oz) quince jelly or paste – if very stiff, soften it in a little warm water

salt and pepper

a little lemon juice

Gillian Temple's Herdwick Tatie Pot

Tatie pot is a standby for every farmer's wife in Cumbria, a good-tempered stew of meat, black pudding and potatoes. Every one has their own variation, and the potatoes may be sliced, cut in chunks or halved for the final layer. This recipe from the Lake District uses Herdwick lamb, typical of the region (see the following page for more about farmhouse produce of this area). Gillian Temple remarks that she makes this dish for hungry farmers returning from gathering sheep on the fells. It's the kind of food which is a necessity when farming in Eskdale, to the west of Hardknott Pass.

Place a layer of meat on the bottom of a casserole. Cover with a layer of carrot, swede and onion, and sprinkle with flour, salt and pepper. Add the rest of the meat, plus the black pudding in a layer. Cover with the remaining swede, carrot and onion, and sprinkle with flour and seasoning. Top the casserole with the sliced potatoes and salt and pepper. Pour the stock over to just below the level of the potato layer. Cover and cook at 190°C, 375°F, Gas mark 5 for at least 3 hours. Remove the lid for the last 30–40 minutes to crisp the potato.

The dish can be kept hot in a low oven for much longer, and will not spoil.

SERVES 6–8

1kg (2¼lb) neck or shoulder of Herdwick lamb, cut into large pieces
200g (7oz) stewing beef, cut into small pieces
4 carrots, chopped
½ a swede, peeled and chopped
1 large onion, chopped
flour, salt and black pepper
200g (7oz) black pudding, sliced
6 large potatoes, sliced
500ml (18fl oz) strong beef stock

Farmhouse Cookery in Cumbria

On a map of Cumbria the Lakes radiate from a central point like spokes of a wheel, with the highest mountains clustered in the middle. East-west routes are difficult, through a few constricted passes, and north-south ones, threaded between lake shores and steep slopes, are not much easier. Even so, tourists have been visiting since the 18th century, attracted by the drama of the scenery. Yet the remoteness of the area, combined with some local pride, managed to keep local distinctiveness alive when it was vanishing elsewhere. The National Trust has been a landowner here for over a century, and is responsible for about a quarter of the land area and the farmsteads on it. Its properties include Townend, a long, low, stone and slate house in the local style, once belonging to a Cumbrian 'statesman' (a farmer who owned his own land), which gives an idea of the traditional way of life in this area. The farming community remains close-knit and was badly affected by the Foot and Mouth epidemic of 2001.

Inevitably, given the height of the hills and their situation on the west coast, the climate is wet and, in winter, often snowy; but it is easy to forget this on a summer's day when the trees are in full leaf, the hills dappled with cloud shadows and the little fields on the flat valley floors full of summer grass. Each lake has its own character: Windermere and Coniston Water are long and narrow, and open to the south; Wastwater is set in a steep, scree-bound valley; Buttermere is almost unbelievably pretty and Ullswater has a feeling of gentle melancholy. Given the lakes and the streams which feed them, one might expect freshwater fish. Sadly, char, once considered a speciality of Windermere, has been overfished and few are now taken. On the coast to the south though, there are brown shrimps which are delicious when simply boiled or potted under spiced butter.

Sheep, especially the native Herdwick, which are mostly confined to this area, graze the tops of the highest hills (see previous page for a recipe that uses local Herdwick lamb). Cattle for beef, and to a lesser extent milk, are also important. On the flatter land which fringes the western edge of the hills, a tradition of pig-keeping and ham-curing flourishes.

This is not country for growing wheat and like much of highland Britain, oats were once important, although the 'clapbread', thin dry oatcakes (that took their name from being 'clapped out' by hand on a flat board), has vanished. Baking traditions include numerous variations on tea breads and other dried fruit-based goodies. Little bread rolls flavoured with caraway, known by the old name of 'wigs', were made in Hawkshead and Kendal. A distinctive and very good gingerbread is made in Grasmere. The Cumbrian tradition of brown sugar, rum and spices, very apparent in sweet foods, is said to be derived from the West India trade once vital to the little ports on the west coast.

Vegetables, beyond plots for domestic use, don't feature, nor is fruit of importance, with the exception of the damson. These little plums were planted in the hedgerows of the valleys draining the southern lakes, and are used for jams and pickles and by one brewery for flavouring beer.

Herdwick sheep at Wastwater in the Lake District, with Yew Barrow in the distance.

Welsh Lamb, Laver and Mutton

Welsh lamb and mutton have been praised for their flavour since the 17th century. George Borrow, the author of *Wild Wales*, remarked on how he dined on an exquisite leg of mutton from the herb-scented pastures of the Berwyn in the 1830s.

Salting mutton legs to produce 'hams' was recorded in several parts of Wales in the past, but no one appears to do this any longer. Lamb or mutton are used in the soup-like stew cawl (see page 28), but roasting seems to have been the favoured method by all who could afford it. Sometimes the joint was wrapped in a huff paste of flour and water to protect it and retain the juices during cooking (a method recorded in Radnor).

Now a co-operative originally established by six National Trust tenants in Snowdonia markets lamb and beef under the name Taste of Snowdonia. Meat is available from both Welsh mountain sheep and crossbreeds. Pure-bred Welsh mountain lamb is distinguished by its smaller size and, many would say, excellent flavour.

To make a huff paste roast, you need a small, lean leg of well-flavoured Welsh lamb; mix the flour with water to make a firm paste, season the leg and wrap it in the paste. Bake at 180°C, 350°F, Gas mark 4 for about 2 hours. Break off the crust and serve the meat with onion sauce (see page 140).

Alternatively, a small shoulder of lamb can be cooked on top of *Tiesen Nionod*, potato and onion baked together (see page 146). Roast lamb or mutton is also good with the south Welsh speciality laver (see page 139).

SERVES 4

1 small lean leg of lamb
plain flour
salt and pepper

Irish Stew

This is a simple dish, but even so it has many variants. Does one add carrots or not? Is it better with or without pearl barley? Should half the potatoes be sliced and added at the start of cooking, to thicken the stew, and the others left whole and added with just enough time to cook at the end? It is one of those dishes with a formula, rather than a recipe, and this one uses twice as much potato by weight as meat, half as much onion, and not too much liquid.

Layer the ingredients in a deep casserole, starting with the meat, adding onion and then potatoes. Sprinkle over the thyme and seasonings, and repeat, finishing with potato. Add a little water or stock and bring to the boil.

Cover tightly, and transfer to the oven at 180°C, 350°F, Gas mark 4 for 2–2½ hours. Check from time to time to ensure that it is not drying up, and add a little more liquid if necessary. The longer and slower the cooking the better, and the stew reheats well.

SERVES 6

1kg (2¼lb) best end or middle
　neck of lamb or mutton,
　cut into chops
500g (about 1lb) onion, thinly
　sliced and roughly chopped
2kg (4½lb) potatoes, peeled and
　sliced about 1cm (½in) thick
1 tablespoon chopped fresh thyme
salt and pepper
1 tablespoon mushroom
　ketchup (optional)
200ml (7fl oz) water or stock

Lamb or Mutton Rogan Josh

Sheep exhibit a fascinating diversity. Small, capable of surviving on high hills but growing fat on lowland grazing, they flourish in environments too harsh for cattle, as well as fitting into a mixed farming economy at lower levels. Many of the breeds now regarded as 'traditional' in the UK owe their origins to the agricultural improvers of the 18th and 19th centuries, who were interested in the quality of both meat and wool.

Several breeds (sometimes called 'primitive' breeds) remained untouched by the improvers. They tend to be small and slower growing and many do not fit well into the grading system used for sheep meat. They include the eye-catching Hebrideans with four horns, goat-like Soay sheep, and Portland sheep (associated with Portland Bill in Dorset).

Tenants on National Trust farms keep a wide range of sheep, including modern, fast-growing commercial stock, traditional British breeds and the small, fine-boned primitive breeds; the environments vary widely, including chalk downlands, coastal grazing and the hills of Wales, Yorkshire and the Lake District. Many direct-market the meat, giving anyone curious about the effect of breed and feed the opportunity to try lamb (and sometimes mutton) from different breeds and environments.

Rogan Josh is not, it could be argued, a traditional dish of farmhouse cookery, although curries have appeared in cookery books since the 18th century. But when mutton fell out of favour in the 1960s, it didn't stop being produced, just found a new market – the Islamic butchers of our cities who buy it as a basis for curries.

Heat the oil in a casserole; add the bay leaves, cinnamon, cardamom pods and cloves and cook gently for 1 minute. Add the shallots and stir well. Cook the mixture slowly for 25 minutes until the shallots are soft and slightly golden. Stir in the garlic and ginger and cook for a few minutes more. Add the meat, salt, chilli and paprika and continue to stir and cook for another 5 minutes or so. Then add the yoghurt and garam masala, mix well and bring to a simmer. If the stew seems on the dry side, add 100ml (3½fl oz) water and stir well.

Cover and transfer to a moderate oven 180°C, 350°F, Gas mark 4 and cook for about 2 hours. Stir occasionally and add a little more water or yoghurt if it seems to be drying. Just before serving, spoon off any excess fat and taste, adding more salt if necessary. Serve with rice or naan bread.

SERVES 6

2 tablespoons vegetable oil
2 bay leaves
2cm (¾in) piece of cinnamon stick
20 green cardamom pods
8 cloves
600g (1¼lb) shallots,
    roughly chopped
6 garlic cloves, crushed
2cm (¾in) piece of fresh root
    ginger, peeled and finely grated
1kg (2¼lb) shoulder of lamb or
    mutton, cut into cubes
1 generous teaspoon salt
2 teaspoons chilli powder
1 tablespoon paprika
500ml (18fl oz) natural
    full-fat yoghurt
2 teaspoons good-quality aromatic
    garam masala

You will need a casserole or pan that can be used on top of the stove and in the oven

Beef, Guinness and Oyster Pie

A dish that shows off the excellent beef available in Northern Ireland. The oysters are a subtle addition to this rich and hearty pie. Oysters can be tricky to open – so if you're nervous, ask your fishmonger to do it for you.

Heat the dripping or oil in a casserole. Add the onion and garlic and fry gently until soft, about 20 minutes. Remove with a slotted spoon and put on one side. Mix the flour, salt and pepper and toss the beef in it. Brown it in the fat left over from frying the onion. Shake in any remaining flour and stir to absorb the fat. Return the onion to the pan and add the beef stock and the Guinness, stirring well. Add the parsley and thyme, cover and transfer to a low oven 150°C, 300°F, Gas mark 2 for 2½–3 hours. When cooked, pour the mixture into a deep pie dish and allow to cool.

Just before cooking the pie, open the oysters and add the flesh and any juices (strained) to the beef mixture. Roll out the pastry to 5mm (¼in) thickness and cover the pie. Scallop the edges with a sharp knife. Cut leaves or other decorations for the top from the pastry trimmings, and glaze the pastry with beaten egg.

Bake at 220°C, 425°F, Gas mark 7 for 20 minutes, then reduce the heat to 180°C, 350°F, Gas mark 4 and bake for a further 30 minutes.

SERVES 6

60g (2oz) dripping or oil
1 large onion, chopped
2 garlic cloves, crushed
4 tablespoons plain flour
1 teaspoon salt and some pepper
750g (1lb 10oz) stewing beef,
   trimmed of all fat and gristle
   and cut into large cubes
400ml (14fl oz) beef stock
300ml (½ pint) Guinness
1 tablespoon chopped fresh thyme
1 tablespoon chopped
   fresh parsley
12 oysters
500g (1lb 2oz) puff pastry
1 egg, beaten, to glaze

Pot Roast Brisket with Summer Vegetables

All those involved with marketing their own farm's meat remark that no one seems to want brisket. Strange, because it has a lovely flavour and makes wonderful gravy, as showcased in this delicious recipe.

Melt a little fat in a casserole and brown the meat all over. Remove and put on one side, add the spring onions and garlic to the fat and cook gently. When they have softened a bit, pour in the red wine and let it boil for a minute or two. Add the carrots and thyme and sit the meat on top. Sprinkle with the salt and pepper. Cover the pot with foil and a lid and cook on a very low heat, or in a low oven at 170°C, 325°F, Gas mark 3, for about 2½ hours.

At this point, uncover the pot. The meat will have produced lots of gravy. Add the peas and beans. Seal the pot again and continue to cook for another 30–40 minutes. Remove the meat to a warm dish. Skim the gravy if it seems to have a lot of fat on top. Combine the cornflour or arrowroot with a little cold water and add to the gravy, bring to the boil and stir while it thickens. Taste and correct the seasoning.

SERVES 4–6

dripping, oil or bacon fat
lkg (2¼lb) brisket, boned
  and rolled
1 bunch spring onions, chopped
1 garlic clove, crushed
150ml (¼ pint) red wine
200g (7oz) young carrots, topped
  and tailed (if they are really
  young, they won't need peeling)
1 sprig thyme
1 teaspoon salt and some pepper
100g (3½oz) shelled fresh peas
150–200g (5–7oz) green beans,
  cut in short lengths
2 teaspoons cornflour or
  arrowroot

Beef in Branscombe Bitter

The National Trust owns the Branscombe Vale Brewery in Devon. I used their Drayman's Best Bitter, a smooth, hoppy beer, for this casserole.

Mix the flour with a scant teaspoon of salt and plenty of black pepper, and turn the beef in it. Heat a frying pan or casserole and cook the bacon gently, adding butter or oil if it doesn't yield much fat. Remove the bacon and brown the meat in the fat. Add the garlic and cook briefly, then the onions, and stir in any remaining flour. Return the bacon to the pan. Add the beer and let it bubble. Stir in the sugar and mustard.

Cook very gently at 150°C, 300°F, Gas mark 2 for 3 hours. The stew is much better left until the next day, when you can lift any solidified fat off the top. Reheat gently and serve with baked potatoes and glazed carrots.

SERVES 4

3 tablespoons plain flour
salt and pepper
600g (1¼lb) shin of beef,
    thickly sliced
2 rashers dry cure bacon,
    cut into matchsticks
30g (1oz) butter or
    2 tablespoons oil
1 garlic clove, crushed
250g (9oz) small onions, peeled
400ml (14fl oz) bitter beer
1 teaspoon brown sugar
½ teaspoon English mustard

Steak and Kidney Pie or Pudding

Mr Bristow, who farms near Redhill, Surrey, on the southern slopes of the North Downs, produces superb quality lamb and Aberdeen Angus beef. Try the latter in this steak and kidney mixture, good in either a pie or a pudding.

Melt a little of the dripping in a large pan and cook the onion gently for about 30 minutes until soft. Remove to a casserole.

Mix 2 tablespoons of the flour with ½ teaspoon of salt and some pepper, and toss the beef and kidney in it. Add the rest of the dripping to the frying pan and brown the meat, in batches if necessary, transferring to the casserole when done. Sprinkle another tablespoon or so of flour into the frying pan to take up any remaining fat and gradually stir in the beef stock, scraping the base of the pan to incorporate all the residues from cooking the meat. It doesn't matter if the mixture includes a few lumps at this stage. Bring to the boil and cook for a few minutes, then pour over the meat. Add the bay leaf, allspice and a splash of Worcestershire sauce. Cover, transfer to the oven and cook at 170°C, 325°F, Gas mark 3 for 2 hours. Taste and add more seasoning if necessary.

Allow to cool and then use either in a pudding (see opposite) or cover with puff pastry for a pie.

SERVES 4–6

40g (1½oz) dripping
1 large onion, chopped
3 tablespoons plain flour
salt and pepper
900g (2lb) stewing beef, trimmed and cut in 2.5cm (1in) cubes
150–200g (5–7oz) ox kidney, trimmed and cut in 1cm (½in) cubes
400ml (14fl oz) beef stock
1 bay leaf
½ teaspoon ground allspice
Worcestershire sauce

You will need a 1.2 litre (2 pint) pudding basin or a pie dish

Combine the flour, suet and a pinch of salt. Add enough water to make a coherent dough. Use this to line the pudding basin.

Form the pastry into a ball and roll out to a circle about 1cm (½in) thick. Cut out a quarter of the circle and set aside. Brush the edges of the pastry with cold water, then ease it into the basin, making a neat seam up the edge where the section was removed. Take the reserved piece of pastry and re-roll it into a small circle. Add the filling to the basin, brush the edge of the smaller circle with water, and use it as a lid, pressing round the edges to seal. Trim the pastry and cover with a double layer of foil or greaseproof paper, with a pleat to allow for the pudding to expand during cooking. Tie securely round the rim of the basin with string and make a loop over the top to form a handle.

Steam for 1½ hours. Pin a napkin round the basin and take it to the table to serve.

FOR THE SUET CRUST
350g (12oz) self-raising flour,
**   plus extra for dusting**
175g (6oz) shredded suet
salt

Roast Beef and Yorkshire Pudding

A family favourite for Sundays and holidays. Buy a handsome joint appropriate to the number of people expected, allow it to come to room temperature before cooking and season it with salt and pepper. Roast in the conventional manner, starting in a hot oven 240°C, 475°F, Gas mark 9 for 15 minutes, and then reducing the temperature to 180°C, 350°F, Gas mark 4 for the rest of the time. Allow 20 minutes per 500g (1lb 2oz) plus 20 minutes extra for medium-cooked meat. Then remove the meat from the oven, put on a hot serving plate and leave to rest for 20–30 minutes while you make the gravy and Yorkshire pudding.

Traditionally, Yorkshire pudding is made in a 24cm (about 9in) square tin, although individual round puddings of 12cm (5in) in diameter work just as well. Mix the eggs, flour and salt, trying to avoid creating lumps. Blend in the milk and water to give a mixture the consistency of thin cream. This is best done a couple of hours ahead of time.

When the beef is out of the oven, turn the heat up to 220°C, 425°F, Gas mark 7. Add a tablespoon of dripping to the tin and heat it in the oven until smoking hot. Pour in all but 2 tablespoons of the batter (this should hiss spectacularly if the fat is the right temperature) and put the pudding in the oven.

Take the tin the beef was roasted in and spoon off any excess fat. Scrape up the sediment using any juices from roasting the meat and make up the amount of liquid to about 200ml (7fl oz) with water or stock (in our household, it would have been water from cooking the vegetables). Let it bubble, then take it off the heat and stir in the reserved Yorkshire pudding batter. Keep stirring until the mixture thickens. Add a little more liquid as appropriate, taste, and adjust the seasoning.

SERVES 6

FOR THE PUDDING
2 eggs
100g (3½oz) plain flour
pinch of salt
250ml (9fl oz) milk and water
    mixed half and half
beef dripping from the roast

FOR THE GRAVY
300ml (½ pint) beef stock
salt and pepper

Staffordshire Steaks

Braised steak recipes of this kind are out of fashion at present, which is a shame as they taste good and can be left to look after themselves in a low oven.

Cut the steak into 2–3 serving pieces. Fry in hot dripping until nicely brown on both sides. Transfer to an ovenproof dish. Fry the onion in the same dripping and add to the steaks. Shake in a little flour to absorb the fat, then add enough boiling water to make a sauce. Add the ketchup, taste and season with pepper and a little salt if necessary. Pour the sauce over the steaks and bake in a low oven at 140°C, 275°F, Gas mark 1 for 2 hours. Serve with creamy mashed potato and crisply fried onions.

SERVES 2–3

500g (1lb 2oz) rump steak
beef dripping
1 large onion, sliced
plain flour for the sauce
250ml (9fl oz) boiling water
2 tablespoons mushroom ketchup
salt and pepper

Meat and Tatie Pies

As made by my grandmother on the family farm in the Yorkshire Dales for baking days, when she needed a dish that would take care of itself most of the time (see the following page for more on typical Yorkshire produce). She wouldn't have added garlic, but it is an improvement.

Put the meat in a deep pie dish. Add the onion, herbs, garlic and season well with pepper and ½ teaspoon salt.

Add the liquid and cover with a butter paper or a piece of buttered foil. Cook at 170°C, 325°F, Gas mark 3 for 1 hour. Remove from the oven and layer the sliced potatoes on top. Season with a little more salt, dot with butter, cover with the paper or foil again and return to the oven for another hour.

At the end of this time, the potatoes will be almost cooked. Remove the dish from the oven and turn the heat up to 190°C, 375°F, Gas mark 5. Discard the paper. Roll out the pastry and put it over the potatoes. Return the pie to the oven for about 20 minutes, just long enough to cook the pastry. Serve with steamed cabbage or broccoli.

SERVES 4–6

750g (1lb 10oz) stewing beef, trimmed of fat and gristle and cut in small slices
1 medium onion, chopped
1 tablespoon each chopped fresh thyme, marjoram and parsley
2 garlic cloves, crushed
salt and pepper
100ml (3½fl oz) water, stock or beef gravy
750g (1lb 10oz) potatoes, peeled and thinly sliced
butter
1 quantity shortcrust pastry made with lard (see page 13)

Farmhouse Cookery in Yorkshire

Yorkshire divides very roughly into a hilly, wet western part and a lower, drier east. In the south-west, the hills are formed of millstone grit and the rocks of the coal measures. Steep, narrow valleys such as Calderdale rise to acid heather moorlands. Traces of the traditional pattern of farming can be seen in the grey gritstone farmsteads which pepper the landscape. The traditional methods of supplementing income from the land – wool processing and weaving, ironworking and coal extraction – gave rise to the industrial towns of the area. Market gardening became important, providing fruit and vegetables for the towns, and early forced rhubarb was a speciality of the Wakefield area.

Further north, the broad glaciated valleys of the rivers Wharfe, Nidd, Ure, Swale and their tributaries provide excellent grazing for sheep and cattle. The underlying limestone makes for a sweet, herb-rich pasture with the classic Dales landscape of grey limestone walls draped over flat valley bottoms, threaded up 'scars' (steep limestone outcrops with flat tops) stretching away across the hill tops, demarcating the grazing land of one parish from another. Cattle grazing these pastures produce excellent milk for cheese-making, a tradition that dates back to the Middle Ages and probably originated with the monks of the great monastic houses at Fountains and Rievaulx. Cheese-making became especially important in Wensleydale, where farmers' wives made semi-hard cheeses in summer, to be kept for Christmas and the winter. Wensleydale cheese is still made, although most of it is produced in creameries. The land becomes bleaker and less populated as one progresses northwards through Swaledale, which gives its name to the local black-faced hill sheep.

To the east of the Pennines, in the flatter land of south Yorkshire and the Vale of York, the rivers wind through areas of deep, rich soil to join the Humber estuary in Humberside. This territory, and the higher Wolds – the rolling chalk hills of eastern Yorkshire – is used for arable crops, especially sugar-beet and barley. The heather-covered North York Moors rise gently from the south and end in a precipitous ironstone scarp, bounding the county to the north. The coastline provides dramatic contrasts; from the high creamy-white cliffs of Flamborough Head, south through the rounded boulder clay shoreline of Holderness to the slender comma of Spurn Point.

In the late 18th and early 19th centuries, the pasturelands of Yorkshire and Durham were renowned for producing cattle of prodigious size: the Craven Heifer, the Airedale Heifer and the Durham Ox are immortalised on numerous pub signs. Yorkshire still produces much good beef (as used in the traditional Yorkshire recipe on the previous page) although it is unlikely to come from Shorthorn cattle, the breed favoured in the past. Beef dripping is used for frying in fish shops and can be bought in large white hunks from local butchers, many of whom also sell traditional potted beef. The native sheep breeds include Swaledales, the closely-related Dalesbreds, and the ringlet-coated Teeswaters and Wensleydales. Pigs were important in the weaving areas of south-west Yorkshire, where the Large White, now an important commercial breed, and the Middle White, rarer, but still favoured in parts of Yorkshire and Lancashire, developed in the 19th century. Ham-curing, using the dry salt cure which eventually became known as the York cure, was also important, and locally produced hams can be bought from a few butchers.

Baking included a tradition of using oatmeal, as the climate and topography of the north are not conducive to growing wheat. In the 19th century, the inhabitants of the West Riding ate havercakes, a distinctive form of oatcake, which requires considerable skill to make properly; sadly, the last commercial maker closed in 1999. Home baking was of considerable importance. The oat tradition appears in parkin, the local version of gingerbread. Wheat bread was also made at home, in large loaves or as flat 'oven bottom cakes', and lightly fruited teacakes. Cakes included 'spice cake' – large fruit loaves made for the tea table, and numerous sponge cakes, buns and pies, including curd tarts. Pastry was more important in the East Riding, where rhubarb or apple pies were served for the farmhands' breakfasts in the early 20th century.

Yockenthwaite Top Farm, Skipton, North Yorkshire.

Carlisle Steak

An updated version of a dish from the Lake District, which Mrs Arthur Webb noted as 'guaranteed to keep out the chilliest cold' when she came across it in the 1930s. She served it with fried potatoes, but I prefer a mixture of mashed potato and parsnip. Well-matured rump steak is best for both flavour and texture. The meat needs 6–12 hours marinating.

Mix the vinegar, soy, sugar, beer and allspice in a wide shallow bowl and put the steaks in it. Cover and put to one side; turn the meat from time to time. When you are ready to cook the meat, lift it out and allow the liquid to drain off it for a few minutes. Reserve the marinade.

Blot the steaks dry with kitchen paper and dust with flour. Heat a smear of oil in a heavy frying pan, and when hot put the steaks in. Allow to sizzle for a few minutes, turn, and continue until they are done to your taste. Remove from the pan and let them rest on a warm plate while you make the sauce. Add the butter to the steak cooking residues. When it has melted, stir in a tablespoon of flour. Add the marinade, stirring well to incorporate the roux and any bits stuck to the pan. Add a little stock or water if it seems too thick. Pour over the steaks and garnish with chopped parsley.

SERVES 4

4 tablespoons malt vinegar
4 tablespoons soy sauce
1 tablespoon muscovado sugar
100ml (3½fl oz) bitter beer
½ teaspoon ground allspice
4 pieces of rump steak
1 tablespoon plain flour,
    plus extra for dusting
oil for frying
30g (1oz) butter
chopped parsley to serve

Escalopes of Pork with Apples and Cider

A recipe for local produce from south-west England inspired by the French Normandy tradition of cream and apples.

Dip the escalopes in the seasoned flour. Melt the butter in a large frying pan. When it foams, add the pork and cook briskly, a couple of minutes per side. Remove to a warm plate. Pour the brandy into the pan, scrape up any sediment, then ignite it and burn off the alcohol. Add the cider and the apple slices. Allow to boil and reduce the cider to a quarter of the original volume (remove the apple slices before this point if they become tender). Add the cream to the pan and stir thoroughly, allowing it to boil. Taste for seasoning. Return the pork and any accumulated juices to the sauce, simmer for a minute or two and serve.

SERVES 4

4 thin pork escalopes
3 tablespoons seasoned flour
30g (1oz) butter
2 tablespoons brandy
100ml (3½fl oz) dry cider
2 apples, peeled, cored and
 thinly sliced
4 tablespoons double cream
salt and pepper

Denise Bell's Slow-Roast Shoulder of Pork

The essential ingredient for this is a very well brought up pig. At Heritage Prime in Dorset (www.heritageprime.co.uk), Denise rears her Tamworths for much longer than conventional farmers, giving very large, well-flavoured joints. To take advantage of this, you need to apply to her well in advance and be prepared to spend on quality. Otherwise, scout round your local farmers' market for someone who raises a traditional breed to a high welfare standard, and buy a piece with a decent covering of fat.

Cooking time depends on size: a whole shoulder weighing 9kg (20lb) takes 24 hours, a piece half that size 16 hours. However, the method works even on a relatively small piece if the cooking time is reduced proportionately. For example, give a piece of boned and rolled shoulder weighing 2kg (4½lb) 6–7 hours in the oven.

Take the pork out of the fridge an hour or two before cooking and allow it to come to room temperature. Preheat the oven to 240°C, 475°F, Gas mark 9. Make sure the skin of the pork is dry before rubbing it with olive oil, salt and fresh thyme; put a few sprigs of thyme underneath as well. Put the pork in the hot oven and leave it for 20–30 minutes. Turn the temperature down to 140°C, 275°F, Gas mark 1 and leave it until almost the end of cooking time (a little longer won't matter). About 30 minutes before eating, turn the oven up to maximum again and give the meat a final blast for 15–20 minutes. The crackling is wonderful and the meat has a melting texture. Serve with a salad of bitter leaves and some good bread.

SERVES 16 OR MORE

1 shoulder of pork
olive oil
salt
fresh thyme

Roast Pork with Ginger and Madeira

This is not a traditional recipe, although the use of Madeira is a nod back to the late 19th century, when it was popular.

Leave the pork on a plate in the fridge overnight, uncovered; this is one way to encourage crisp crackling. Shortly before cooking remove it from the fridge, rub the skin with a little olive oil and sprinkle with salt. Put the ginger and garlic in a roasting tin and place the pork on top (try to ensure it covers them, otherwise they burn). Heat the oven to 220°C, 425°F, Gas mark 7 and put the meat in. Roast at this temperature for 30 minutes, then add most of the Madeira to the tin and turn the heat down to 150°C, 300°F, Gas mark 2. Leave it to cook gently for another 2–2½ hours. Check occasionally to make sure it's not drying out (if it burns, it will taste bitter). Add the rest of the Madeira halfway through the cooking time.

When the meat is well cooked, lift it out of the tin to rest in a warm place. Drain the cooking juices into a bowl and pick out the garlic cloves. Spoon off as much fat as possible, returning a tablespoon to the roasting tin. Add the flour and mix well over a low heat. Pour in the cooking juices and stir well, scraping in any sediment from the edges of the tin. Simmer until it thickens a little, and stir in the stock. Taste, correct the seasoning, and serve with some creamy mashed parsnip.

SERVES 6

1.5kg (3¼lb) belly pork, the
  skin scored for roasting
olive oil
salt and pepper
20g (¾oz) root ginger, peeled,
  cut into matchsticks
2–3 garlic cloves, bruised
  but not peeled
6 tablespoons Madeira
1 dessertspoon plain flour
250ml (9fl oz) chicken stock

Cumberland Sausage in Beer

Cumberland sausages are a Lake District tradition. They should be full of coarse-cut meat and a bit of seasoning, and come in one long coil, not as links. They are excellent grilled or fried, but cooking them in beer produces a good gravy.

Melt the dripping or oil and cook the sausage briefly on both sides, just enough to brown it. Remove it to a plate and add the onion to the fat and cook gently until soft but not brown. Sprinkle in the flour and stir well. Stir in the beer. Let it bubble and reduce a little. Add the sausage and cook very gently for 30–40 minutes. Taste the gravy and season if necessary, but the sausage will probably have provided enough salt. Serve with mashed potatoes.

SERVES 4

30g (1oz) beef dripping or
  2 tablespoons oil
500–600g (about 1–1¼lb)
  Cumberland sausage
  in a long piece
1 onion, sliced
1 tablespoon plain flour
300ml (½ pint) beer,
  preferably not too bitter
salt and pepper

Try to use a frying pan or casserole in which the sausage will fit in a neat coil.

Pease Pudding and Ham

Very much a north-eastern tradition, pease pudding can be bought in butchers' shops in Northumberland and Durham ready for heating up. This recipe is for those who have to start from scratch.

Soak the ham and the peas separately overnight. The next day, drain both and put them in a pan, adding the onions and enough fresh water to cover. Simmer gently for 2 hours, by which time the peas should be a purée and the ham thoroughly cooked. Remove the ham and allow to cool.

To make the peas into a pudding, mix together the pea purée, butter and egg. Season well.

Pour into a greased pudding basin and steam for an hour. Turn out and serve with the boiled ham shank.

SERVES 6

1 ham shank
450g (1lb) yellow split peas
2 onions, finely chopped
30g (1oz) butter
1 egg
salt and pepper

Stuffed Pork Fillet

A recipe sent from Northern Ireland to Florence White, when she was collecting recipes in the 1920s.

To make the stuffing, cook the onion gently in the butter. Mix it with the breadcrumbs and herbs and season with salt and pepper. Bind with milk.

Cut the pork fillet obliquely to give thin slices. If these don't seem to have a very large surface area, put them between sheets of baking parchment and beat them out a little with a rolling pin or cutlet bat. Divide the stuffing between them, and roll each slice up, securing the roll with a cocktail stick or tying with kitchen string.

Butter an ovenproof dish that will hold the rolls of pork neatly and place them in it. Dust over with flour and dot with a little more butter. Cook at 200°C, 400°F, Gas mark 6 for 15–20 minutes.

Remove the cooked pork from the dish and keep warm. Add a little more butter to the cooking residues, and a dusting of flour. Deglaze with stock, wine or water to make a little gravy. Serve with mashed potatoes and apple sauce.

SERVES 4

600–700g (1¼lb–1½lb) pork fillet

FOR THE STUFFING
60g (2oz) onion, finely chopped
30g (1oz) butter
120g (4oz) white breadcrumbs
3 teaspoons chopped fresh sage
3 teaspoons chopped fresh parsley
salt and pepper
a little milk
a little butter
plain flour
stock, wine or water, for the gravy

Devilled Chicken

Surrey and Sussex were famous for chickens and capons up until the Second World War; they were expensive and considered a treat. 'Devilling' poultry or game in a spicy sauce was popular in the 19th and early 20th centuries.

Season the chicken with salt and cook under a hot grill, turning frequently, until the juices run clear when the thickest part is pierced with a skewer. The chicken can be baked, but will not be as succulent.

Mix the cream, curry powder and mustard in a frying pan. Add the pieces of chicken and any meaty juices from the grill pan. Heat gently; the mixture will thicken as it comes to the boil. Serve with boiled rice.

SERVES 4–6

1 chicken, jointed
salt
300ml (½ pint) single cream
1 tablespoon Madras curry powder
1 tablespoon dry mustard powder

Chicken and Parsley Pie

Until quite recently, most farms and country smallholders kept a few hens. They scratched around the barnyard, looking for seeds, grains and insects. Often, the birds were quite ornamental, chosen for the colours and textures of their plumage as much as anything, but they still had to earn their living. Eggs were vital to the farm economy, their sale providing income for the farmer's wife. At times of the year when eggs were plentiful they were used for all sorts of dishes, including preserves such as lemon curd (see page 280).

Chickens also provided meat, either for sale or for the pot. Every clutch of eggs hatched was statistically likely to contain an equal number of hens and cockerels, and most of the latter were killed for the pot as soon as they were big enough. Old laying hens, too, ended up in the kitchen as stews or stocks.

Some farms also kept turkeys, ducks or geese, but these were considered a little more specialised and their presence was dictated more by individual tastes and regional habits – although it was always admitted that two or three geese made the best possible watchdogs, as they were intensely vocal whenever disturbed and intimidating to anyone unused to them.

Versions of the dish given here were recorded in both Devon and Cornwall, always, it seems, as very large pies made from two chickens. Delicious both hot and cold. You can ask your butcher to joint the chicken for you.

Season the chicken with pepper, salt and a scrape of nutmeg. Dust with flour. Put a layer of parsley and some shallot in the pie dish, and cover with chicken pieces. Scatter the ham or bacon and the remaining parsley and shallot over, then fill up the dish with chicken. Insert the pie funnel in the middle. Add the stock to fill up the dish to about the halfway mark. Roll out the pastry and cover the pie. Make a hole in the centre to accommodate the pie funnel, and a pastry rose to cover it.

Bake at 220°C, 425°F, Gas mark 7 for 20 minutes, then reduce the heat to 170–180°C, 325–350°F, Gas mark 3–4 and cook for another 1–1¼ hours. At the end of the cooking time, heat the cream to boiling. Ease off the pastry rose and pour into the pie. Serve very hot, or allow to go completely cold and chill.

SERVES 8

2 chickens, the meat cut off, skinned and divided into neat joints (use the carcass and skin to make stock, a little of which is needed for the pie).
salt, pepper and nutmeg
flour for dusting
1 large bunch parsley, stems picked off, chopped
4 shallots, finely chopped
100g (3½oz) cooked ham or bacon, cut in dice
250ml (9fl oz) chicken stock
2 quantities of shortcrust pastry (see page 13)
250ml (9fl oz) double cream

You will need a large deep pie dish and a pie funnel

Chicken Pudding

Savoury puddings were a feature of the cookery of Sussex and Kent in the 19th century. Fillings included mutton and oysters, partridges, and a chicken and ham version from Staplehurst in Kent. They should really be made by putting uncooked meat into the crust and boiling or steaming for several hours, and belong to the days of monster iron ranges, always hot and demanding the constant presence of the farmer's wife or a servant to make sure they weren't boiling dry. This version has been adapted to cut the steaming time.

Flour the chicken. Melt the butter in a large frying pan and add the chicken pieces. Fry gently, turning from time to time, until golden brown on all sides. Add the stock, cover and simmer gently for 40 minutes, then allow to cool slightly. Season rather highly with salt and add the pepper, tarragon and parsley.

SERVES 4–6

1 chicken, skinned and boned,
   cut into large pieces
plain flour to coat
butter for frying
450ml (¾ pint) good chicken stock
salt and pepper
1 tablespoon chopped
   fresh tarragon
1 tablespoon chopped
   fresh parsley
100g (3½oz) well-flavoured
   cooked ham, cut in strips
100g (3½oz) button mushrooms,
   wiped and chopped

Meanwhile, make the suet pastry by combining the breadcrumbs, flour, salt, lemon zest and suet. Add enough water to make a coherent dough and line the basin (see page 93). Lift the chicken out of the cooking liquid and layer it, the ham and the mushrooms in the lined basin. Pour the cooking liquid over the meat and cover with the pastry lid.

Take a large double piece of foil or greaseproof paper, make a generous pleat in the middle and cover the top of the basin with it, remembering that the pudding will expand a little as it cooks. Tie a piece of string round the rim of the basin to hold the foil in place, and take the string across the top of the basin to make a handle.

Lower the covered pudding into boiling water and cook steadily for 1½ hours, adding more boiling water if it shows signs of boiling dry. Pin a napkin round the basin when you take it to the table and serve.

FOR THE SUET CRUST
100g (3½oz) fresh white breadcrumbs
200g (7oz) self-raising flour
½ teaspoon salt
1 teaspoon grated lemon zest
120g (4oz) shredded suet

You will need a 1.2 litre (2 pint) pudding basin and a saucepan large enough to hold it and a quantity of boiling water

Turkey Escalopes with Lemon and Thyme

Lemon zest and thyme are traditional flavourings for many meat stuffings in English cookery; they work well in this coating for escalopes.

Mix the thyme, lemon zest, seasoning and breadcrumbs. Break the egg into a wide bowl and beat lightly. Dip both sides of each escalope in egg and then coat with the breadcrumb mixture. Heat a little butter in a large frying pan and fry the escalopes gently for 3–4 minutes on each side. You may have to do this in batches – keep the cooked escalopes warm in a low oven. Serve with lemon quarters to squeeze over, and watercress or a green salad.

SERVES 4

2 teaspoons chopped fresh thyme
2 teaspoons finely grated
   lemon zest
salt and pepper
120g (4oz) fresh white
   breadcrumbs
1 egg, beaten
4 turkey escalopes, each
   weighing 80–100g (3–3½oz)
butter for frying
lemon quarters to serve

Partridge Pudding

Another salute to the south-eastern tradition of puddings that are typical of the garden of England (see the following page for more information on farmhouse produce from this area). Using raw partridges preserves their delicious flavour, but the pudding needs several hours steaming.

Firstly skin and joint the partridges, or ask your butcher to do it for you. Use the carcasses with a bouquet garni, an onion and a carrot to make a little stock.

To make the pudding, combine the flour, suet and a pinch of salt, and add enough water to make a coherent dough. Use this to line the pudding basin (see page 93). Put the sliced steak in the bottom and then put in the partridge joints and sliced mushrooms in layers, sprinkling salt, pepper and chopped herbs in between. Mix the wine with the partridge stock and pour over the filling. Cover the pudding with the pastry lid and then cover with pleated foil or greaseproof paper. Tie well and steam for at least 3 hours, checking occasionally and topping up the pan with boiling water if necessary. Pin a napkin round the basin before serving.

SERVES 4

2 partridges
350g (12oz) self-raising flour,
    plus extra for dusting
150g (5oz) shredded suet
salt and pepper
150g (5oz) rump steak,
    thinly sliced
100g (3½oz) mushrooms, sliced
1 tablespoon chopped
    fresh parsley
1 tablespoon chopped fresh thyme
100ml (3½fl oz) red wine

You will need a 1.2 litre (2 pint) pudding basin

Farmhouse Cookery in the Garden of England

As the term 'garden of England' suggests, growing fruit and vegetables has been important in the south-eastern corner of England for centuries, and in places the landscape does have a minutely tended feel. Not that it was ever entirely 'garden'. The south coast – Hampshire, Sussex and Kent – includes the high, bare chalk hills of the South Downs, which run from Winchester and end abruptly at Beachy Head almost 100 miles to the east. The chalk reappears as the Isle of Wight. The northern edge of these counties is marked by the dramatic ridge of the North Downs, which meet the sea at Dover. The landscape between the two ranges of hills is sometimes flat clay-filled valleys, at other times undulating and hilly, and by no means all cultivated. To the west of London, chalk rolls through Salisbury Plain and the Marlborough Downs, and also appears to the north in the Chilterns.

The South Downs were famous in the past for grazing huge flocks of sheep, leading to a characteristic close-cropped grass sward. In recent years, the Downs have changed, with some land being ploughed and some reverting to scrub as the number of grazing sheep has diminished. Sheep-grazing was also important on the Levels of Pevensey and Romney Marsh. Traditional animal breeds in the area include Romneys and various breeds of downland sheep; Southdowns were famous in the 19th century as providers of the mutton so important to the Victorian kitchen. Poultry-rearing was of great consequence in Sussex and Surrey up until the Second World War.

Inland, perhaps the strongest distinguishing feature of much of the land between the Downs is the presence of trees, although the great storm of 1987 felled many of the older ones. The word 'forest', from the New Forest on the western edge of Hampshire through to Lyminge Forest in east Kent, actually indicates trees interspersed with areas of heath. Being in the south does not mean a consistently warmer, easier climate, and although summers are hotter and drier than in much of Britain, the eastern part of Kent tends to catch cold easterly winds and snow in winter.

The constraints of modern agriculture and competition from abroad have possibly made the area less of a garden than it once was. Watercress is a special crop, grown in the clear water of springs which emerge at the junction of chalk and clay strata; Hampshire is the principal watercress-growing county in the UK. Some farmers have experimented with more novel crops, such as garlic on the Isle of Wight and, in the sheltered environment of a former walled garden at Slindon near Arundel, pumpkins and squashes. Fruit-growing gives a special character to the high Weald of Kent and Sussex, and is also important in an area to the north-west of London. England's favourite apple, the Cox's Orange Pippin, does well in this climate. Plums and cherries also grow happily, and Kent has a few commercial producers of hazelnuts. Kent's other major crop, hops, is not as important as it used to be, but evidence remains in the oast houses, with their conical roofs and white air vents essential for hop-drying. Soft fruit is also grown, and Hampshire is noted for its early strawberries.

The food of much of south-east England has lost much of its special character under the onslaught of metropolitan influence. Until the Second World War, a distinguishing feature seems to have been the use of suet crust in savoury and sweet puddings. Just as it is said that a Cornishwoman will put anything in a pasty, so it seems that housewives from the south-east made puddings (for a typical pudding recipe of this area, see the previous page). In poor households they might be plain, served with gravy or syrup as rib-sticking food for large and hungry families; in better-off establishments they included meat, sometimes game, or fruit. Home-baking was less important than in some areas, due partly to an 18th- and 19th-century shortage of fuel for wood-fired ovens – some of the woodland cover was planted relatively recently. However, the south-east shared the general British tradition of the cottage pig, making hams, bacon, sausages and 'flead cake', a local variation of the lardy cake.

Hay bales in the fields surrounding Sissinghurst Castle, near Cranbrook, Kent.

Roast Goose with Sage and Onion

At Saltash, on the banks of the River Tamar in Cornwall, Mr and Mrs Hunn rear geese and turkeys for Christmas. The recipe given here is the classic English way with geese. Ask your butcher to retain the giblets, but exclude the liver when making gravy. Fry it in butter, whizz up in a blender and season for a little pâté to eat while the bird roasts.

To make the stuffing, mix the onion and the sage leaves with the breadcrumbs. Add the salt and lemon zest and grind in plenty of pepper. Use the egg to bind the mixture. Remove any visible lumps of fat from inside the goose (render them down for roasting potatoes) and spoon in the stuffing.

Put the goose on a wire rack in a large roasting tin and rub the skin with salt. Roast at 200°C, 400°F, Gas mark 6 for 2½–3 hours, occasionally pouring off the fat which accumulates in the roasting tin.

SERVES 6

1 goose with giblets, weighing
   about 4.5kg (10lb)

FOR THE STUFFING

1 large onion, finely chopped

80g (3oz) fresh sage leaves, finely
   chopped

300g (10½oz) fresh white
   breadcrumbs

1 teaspoon salt

grated zest of ½ lemon

generous amount of freshly
   ground black pepper

1 egg

To make the gravy, cook the bacon gently until the fat runs. Add the vegetables and the giblets and cook until browned, then add the bay leaf, cover with water and leave to simmer gently, allowing the liquid to reduce by about a third.

When the goose is cooked, remove it to a warm plate and leave to rest. Pour off the fat from the roasting tin. Add the brandy and let it bubble, scraping up any sediment. Strain in the stock from the giblets and bring to the boil. Taste and adjust the seasoning. Mix a generous teaspoon of cornflour with a little water and stir into the gravy, heating again until the mixture has thickened.

FOR THE GRAVY
2 rashers bacon, cut in strips
½ onion, chopped
1 carrot, chopped
2 sticks celery, chopped
goose giblets, excluding the liver
1 bay leaf
75ml (2½fl oz) brandy
1 heaped teaspoon cornflour

Salt Duck

A dish considered traditional to Welsh cookery. Although an early recipe for this suggests serving it hot with onion sauce, it is also delicious cold, carved thinly and served with a salad of oranges.

SERVES 4

1 duck
100g (3½oz) salt

Rub the duck all over with salt and put in a deep pottery dish or other non-reactive container. Store in a cool place. Turn and rub the salt in twice a day for 3 days.

To cook, rinse off the excess salt and cover the duck with cold water. Simmer very gently for 2 hours.

Serve hot or cold, or with onion sauce (see page 140) as desired.

Wood Pigeon Stew

Wood pigeons gorge on grain crops. Unusually for game, they are available all year round and make a good late-summer ragout. This recipe from Hampshire originally used whole birds – if you want to do this, braise them gently for about an hour. You can ask your butcher to prepare the birds for you – make sure you retain the carcasses for making stock, which could be used in this recipe.

Melt the butter in a casserole that can be used on the hob and add the bacon and mushrooms. Cook gently together until the bacon fat is translucent and has yielded much of its fat. Remove the bacon and mushrooms with a slotted spoon. Dust the pigeon breasts with flour and fry gently in the bacon fat until brown on both sides, then put to one side with the bacon and mushrooms. Add a little more flour to the remaining fat and stir to make a roux. Stir in the stock to make a smooth sauce and add the mushroom ketchup. Put the bacon and mushrooms back in the sauce and add the peas (frozen ones work just as well as fresh). Place the pigeon breasts on top.

Stew gently on the top of the stove for about 25 minutes, turning the pigeon breasts occasionally – they should be almost cooked, with a trace of pink at the centre. Taste the sauce and add salt, pepper and lemon juice to taste. Allow to rest for 5 minutes and serve with new potatoes.

SERVES 4

30g (1oz) butter
100g (3½oz) fatty bacon,
    cut in strips
200g (7oz) button mushrooms,
    sliced
4 oven-ready wood pigeons,
    skinned and breasts removed
plain flour, for dusting
400ml (14fl oz) stock – use the
    pigeon bones or chicken or
    beef stock
2 tablespoons mushroom ketchup
200–250g (7–9oz) shelled peas
salt and pepper
lemon juice

Hare Stew

A recipe for using an older animal, this is based on the idea of 'jugging' a hare, which originally meant cooking it in a large deep pot in a bain-marie for several hours, before using the animal's blood to thicken the sauce. As an alternative you can work butter and flour into a paste for this recipe.

The hare should arrive complete with the pluck – kidneys, heart, lungs and liver. This can be cooked with the hare, or the liver reserved, mashed, and added to the sauce at the end of cooking, with the blood.

Scatter the ham or bacon in a casserole and put the hare on top. Add the bouquet, a teaspoon of salt, some pepper and ground mace, the lemon zest, juniper berries and stock. Cover with foil, then the lid of the casserole. Cook at 170°C, 325°F, Gas mark 3 for 3 hours; then add the wine or port and cook for another 1½ hours or so, until the meat is tender. Taste the juices, adding more salt as necessary and a tablespoon or so of redcurrant jelly.

To thicken the sauce, if using the blood, mix with a little of the cooking liquid, then add it to the pot and stir gently over heat without boiling (the sauce will curdle if it boils). Otherwise, add the butter and flour mixture in little pieces and stir to incorporate them. Heat gently until the sauce thickens. Serve with baked potatoes or Norfolk Dumplings (see page 124) as shown opposite.

A WHOLE HARE WILL EASILY SERVE 6

1 hare, cleaned and jointed
200g (7oz) well-flavoured ham or bacon, chopped
bouquet garni of parsley, thyme, marjoram and a bay leaf
salt, pepper and ground mace
1 teaspoon grated lemon zest
2–3 juniper berries, bruised
400ml (14fl oz) well-flavoured stock, preferably beef
150ml (¼ pint) red wine or port
redcurrant jelly
blood of the hare or 30g (1oz) butter and 1 tablespoon plain flour, worked together into a paste

Norfolk Dumplings

The memoirs of Martha Blomfield, who grew up on a Norfolk farm in the late 19th century, inspired me to try the combination of hare stew and dumplings. The dumplings were eaten as a first course with the hare gravy, followed by the meat with numerous vegetables.

Add the yeast to the water and allow it to froth. Mix with the flour and salt, just as if making bread. When the dough is well kneaded, allow it to rise for about an hour.

Have a large pot of boiling salted water at the ready. Divide the dough into 6, make into balls and drop in the water. Keep them boiling for 20–25 minutes. The dumplings will expand a little as they cook. Drain and serve with the hare gravy; don't try to cut them, but pull apart with two forks.

MAKES 6 LARGE DUMPLINGS

1 teaspoon dried yeast
150ml (¼ pint) hand-hot water
250g (9oz) plain flour, plus
    extra for dusting
1 scant teaspoon salt

Venison Bourguignon

Several National Trust estates in the counties bordering Wales produce venison. At Attingham Park, a herd of fallow deer graces Humphry Repton's landscape, and their meat is available in limited quantities through the winter months. It responds well to *boeuf à la Bourguignon* treatment. This recipe is not a traditional British farmhouse recipe, but it is very good. Although it takes a relatively long time to cook, I think it tastes as good or better made in advance and reheated.

Put the venison, onion, garlic, juniper berries, wine and a tablespoon of olive oil in a bowl, plus a scant teaspoon of salt and a generous grind of pepper. Cover and leave to marinate overnight.

The next day, tip the meat into a sieve over a bowl and allow to drain, reserving the marinade. Melt the dripping (or use a little more olive oil) in a heavy casserole and add the bacon. Cook gently and remove when it shows signs of crisping. Cook the mushrooms in the same fat until soft. Lift out with a slotted spoon and put aside with the bacon.

Toss the drained venison (don't worry too much about disentangling the onion) in the flour and brown it in the fat. Add the marinade and stir well, then pour in the stock, stirring while the mixture comes to the boil. Put the bouquet garni in among the meat, cover, and transfer to a low oven, 140–150°C, 275–300°F, Gas mark 1–2 for about 3 hours. Towards the end of cooking, stir in the bacon and mushrooms and check the seasoning. Serve with jacket potatoes or some papardelle pasta, tossed with a little butter and chopped parsley.

SERVES 6–8

900g (2lb) stewing venison, cut in slices 8 x 8cm (3¼ x 3¼in) and 5mm (¼in) thick

1 onion, sliced

1 garlic clove, crushed

4–6 juniper berries, bruised

100ml (3½fl oz) red wine

olive oil

salt and pepper

30g (1oz) beef dripping

4 rashers unsmoked bacon, cut in strips

250g (9oz) button mushrooms, washed, trimmed and sliced

1 tablespoon plain flour

300ml (½ pint) beef stock

bouquet garni of parsley, thyme, marjoram, a bay leaf and a strip of orange peel

Venison Steaks with Allspice, Juniper Berries and Sloe Gin

In the past, venison was a highly prized food of the nobility, and deer stalking in the Scottish Highlands still has an image as an exclusive sport. But red deer are now farmed in several places, and the population of roe and fallow deer has expanded, making this low-fat, flavoursome meat easier and cheaper to buy. Juniper, an excellent flavouring for this meat, was once a common bush across much of Scotland.

Heat the butter and olive oil together in a heavy frying pan. Add the steaks and cook quickly, for 3–4 minutes on each side, depending on thickness. Venison is best on the rare side when cooked this way; don't overdo, or the meat will be tough. Remove to a warm serving dish and keep hot.

Add the sloe gin to the pan and allow to bubble, then add the juniper, allspice and the stock. Cook rapidly until only 3 or 4 tablespoons of liquid remain in the pan. Stir in the cream, adjust the seasoning and serve with the vension steaks. A dish of new potatoes and some French beans are good with this.

SERVES 4

15g (½oz) butter
1 tablespoon olive oil
4 venison steaks, each weighing about 120g (4oz)
about 4 tablespoons sloe gin
6 juniper berries, bruised
a generous pinch ground allspice
about 125ml (5fl oz) stock (venison for preference)
4–6 tablespoons thick cream
salt and pepper

Kidneys in Onions

A dish recorded on the south coast and Isle of Wight in the early to mid-20th century. Well-flavoured beef stock is essential.

Peel the onions, slicing off the root end so they will stand level, and trimming any papery bits from the stem end. Cut a 'lid' off the top of each one and keep on one side. Hollow out the top of each onion so that a kidney will fit inside neatly. Season the insides with a little salt, a dusting of allspice and a little chopped parsley. Nestle the kidneys into the hollows, put the lids on and put a bay leaf on top of each onion, spearing it in place with a clove. Put the onions in a heavy pan or casserole in which they fit neatly and add the stock. Put the lid on, bring to the boil, and then simmer very gently for 1½ hours.

Add the rum and simmer for another 30 minutes, allowing the stock to reduce a little. Taste the stock and adjust the seasoning. Serve in soup bowls, with a spoon and fork, and some good bread to mop up the liquid.

SERVES 4

4 large onions
4 sheep's kidneys
salt
ground allspice
chopped fresh parsley
4 bay leaves
4 cloves
450ml (¾ pint) beef stock
60ml (2fl oz) rum

Ffagod

Also known as faggots, this recipe is one way of dealing with some of the less glamorous bits of pig, typical of South Wales and south-west England. Caul is a thin membrane with a lacy pattern of fat, which lines the stomach cavity of the animal; it wraps the mixture neatly, adds flavour and looks pretty. This recipe is from Glamorgan, and like many Welsh variants uses only liver and includes apple.

Mince or process the onion, apple and liver. Mix with the breadcrumbs, suet, sage, salt and pepper. Soak the caul in a bowl of warm water. After a few minutes it should be soft and easy to spread out. Using scissors, cut 12 neat squares from it, avoiding the fattiest bits. Divide the liver mixture into 12 and wrap each in a piece of the caul. Place in a greased ovenproof dish and add a little stock. Bake at 180°C, 350°F, Gas mark 4 for about an hour.

SERVES 4

200g (7oz) onion, cut in chunks
200g (7oz) cooking apple, peeled and cored
200g (7oz) pig's liver, cut in chunks
200g (7oz) fresh breadcrumbs
60g (2oz) shredded suet
20 sage leaves, shredded
1 teaspoon salt and some pepper
1 pig's caul
250ml (9fl oz) stock

Lamb or Mutton Liver with Oranges and Tomatoes

We seem to have lost the trick of using offal. In the past, it would have been considered wasteful not to use every edible bit of an animal – although items such as tripe and chitterlings were mostly thought of as food for the poor.

The time when most rural people were likely to have to cope with this was when a pig had been killed for family consumption. This made an enormous amount of work, as the insides had to be prepared for use as sausage casings, made into faggots or haslet (a type of meatloaf), and the fat rendered for lard. The sides and hind legs were salted to make bacon and ham. Even so, there was far more fresh meat awaiting use than the average family could eat, so in the days before refrigeration, the custom of 'pig cheer' was observed: plates of meat and offal were made up and taken as presents to neighbours, who responded in kind when they themselves came to kill a pig.

Customs associated with killing sheep are less obvious, perhaps because these animals are generally smaller than pigs; but it would still have been seen as a virtue to use as much of the insides as possible, and the Scottish tradition of haggis, made from the pluck of a sheep, chopped, seasoned and mixed with oatmeal, stuffed into the cleaned stomach, is an example of this.

'Oranges don't grow in England,' said Adam Simon at Tamarisk Farm in Dorset when we discussed the best way to cook liver, which he sells along with the meat from his sheep flock. True. But then tomatoes, his preferred accompaniment, are not native to the British countryside either.

Heat the dripping or oil in a frying pan and fry the onion fairly briskly for 10 minutes, stirring from time to time.

Mix the flour with the paprika, cumin, salt and pepper and turn the liver slices in it. Move the onion to one side of the pan and add the liver, turning the slices to brown them on both sides. Then add the tomatoes, the orange zest and juice and a little water if the mixture seems on the dry side. Simmer gently until the liver is done to your taste – opinions vary as to whether it should be pink in the middle or well cooked.

SERVES 4

dripping or oil
1 large onion, chopped
1 tablespoon plain flour
1 teaspoon paprika
½ teaspoon ground cumin
½ teaspoon salt and pepper
400g (14oz) mutton or lamb liver, cut into thin slices
4 tomatoes, skinned, deseeded and diced
1 teaspoon grated orange zest plus the juice of a whole orange

Sauces, Sides and Vegetables

Sauces

Celery Sauce for Boiled Turkey

Most people think of roast when they cook turkey, but the bird is good boiled as well. If you want to try this, simmer a small turkey – about 5kg (11lb) – in water with the usual potherbs (leeks, carrots and onions), for about 1½ hours. When it's done, the leg will start to part easily from the body. Alternatively, try the sauce with some slices of leftover cooked turkey gently reheated in it.

To make the sauce, simmer the celery in the stock for about 20 minutes. Knead the butter and flour together and add to the stock and celery in small bits. Stir well, keeping the temperature just below boiling, until the mixture thickens. Add the cream and season with salt and pepper, and a little chopped tarragon if you like.

SERVES 6–8

1 head of celery, trimmed, leaves
    removed, thinly sliced
850ml (1½ pints) light stock
    (made from veal, chicken
    or the turkey giblets)
60g (2oz) butter, softened
40g (1½oz) plain flour
100ml (3½fl oz) single cream
salt and pepper
fresh tarragon, chopped (optional)

Salad Sauce

An old-fashioned salad dressing of the sort made in many country houses and large farmhouses during the 19th century. Delicious with freshly gathered, crisp, green lettuce hearts.

Pound the egg yolks and onion together in a mortar. When smooth, add the salt, mustard and cider vinegar. Mix well. Add the oil a little at a time, then mix in the cream. Stir in a few drops of herb-flavoured vinegar, and a little ketchup or Worcestershire sauce if desired. Taste and adjust the seasoning as necessary.

SERVES 4–6

2 hard-boiled egg yolks
1 teaspoon very finely
    chopped onion
pinch of salt
¼ teaspoon mustard powder
1 tablespoon cider vinegar
2 generous tablespoons olive oil
2 tablespoons single cream
herb-flavoured vinegar (tarragon
    or basil)
mushroom ketchup or
    Worcestershire sauce (optional)

Watercress Sauce for Salmon or Trout

Layers of chalk and clay in a landscape, such as Dorset and Hampshire, give springs of pure water. Clean water is the best environment for growing watercress. If you're lucky, it also means good streams for trout fishing.

Strip the leaves from the watercress and reserve. Chop the stalks and cook gently in the water or stock until just soft. Make a roux with the butter and flour, and strain in the cooking liquid (discard the stalks). Cook gently, stirring constantly, until the sauce thickens. Stir in the cream and adjust the seasoning, adding a squeeze of lemon juice to taste. Finally add the reserved leaves and serve immediately with eggs or fish, such as poached salmon or river trout.

SERVES 4–6

1 bunch watercress
300ml (½ pint) water or fish stock
30g (1oz) butter
30g (1oz) plain flour
1 tablespoon double cream
salt and pepper
squeeze of lemon juice

Watercress Butter

Special-occasion teas for birthdays, cricket matches, or visits by groups such as the W.I. required mountains of pre-cut sandwiches with fillings of meat, eggs or flavoured butters. This watercress butter is also good with fish such as trout or cod.

60g (2oz) butter
1 bunch watercress, leaves
   only, finely chopped
pinch of salt and pepper
squeeze of lemon juice

Cream the butter, add the watercress and season to taste with salt, pepper and lemon juice.

Use as a spread for sandwiches, especially with ham or tongue, or serve melting over grilled fish or poached eggs.

Laver Sauce

Laver, gathered from the Glamorgan and
Pembroke coasts and prepared by long, gentle
cooking, is sold in local markets in south Wales.
It looks rather unpromising, a dark brown sludge,
but it makes an excellent sauce for Welsh lamb
and mutton, especially that grazed on the salt
marshes around the Welsh coast.

Heat the laver gently with the butter and season to taste
with orange juice, salt and pepper. If Seville oranges are
not in season, use lemon or tangerine juice. Serve very hot.

SERVES 6

450g (1lb) prepared laver
80g (3oz) butter
juice of 1 Seville orange
salt and pepper

Onion Sauce

This Welsh sauce is a traditional accompaniment for hot salt duck (see page 120), roast lamb or mutton.

Put the onions and milk in a pan with a little of the butter and cook very gently until the onions are almost a purée. In a separate pan, melt the rest of the butter and add the flour. Stir in the onion purée and bring to the boil. Season, adding a dust of sugar if the onions seem to lack sweetness, and stir in the cream. Serve hot.

SERVES 4–6

2 large onions, sliced
150ml (¼ pint) milk
30g (1oz) butter
1 tablespoon plain flour
salt, pepper and a little sugar
2–3 tablespoons double cream

Venison Sauce

A little care is needed when roasting venison because the meat tends to dry out. Use haunch or saddle. It is worth taking the trouble to lard it (using a special larding needle to insert small pieces of pork back fat under the surface of the meat at regular intervals). Cook for 15–20 minutes at 200°C, 400°F, Gas mark 6 per 500g (1lb 2oz). Baste frequently and allow it to rest before carving. Serve it with this old-fashioned but good late 19th-century sauce derived from the haute cuisine tradition.

Melt the butter in a large frying pan and add the onion, bacon, celery, cloves, peppercorns, thyme and the bay leaf. Fry briskly, stirring frequently, until the vegetables are golden brown. Stir in the flour, then the stock and simmer for an hour.

Strain the contents of the pan into a bowl, pressing to extract as much flavour as possible. Return the liquid to the pan and add the redcurrant jelly. In a separate pan, boil the wine until it is reduced to about 2 tablespoons, and stir into the sauce. Cook gently for a few minutes, check the seasoning and serve very hot with a roast of venison.

SERVES 6

60g (2oz) butter
½ large onion, sliced
2 rashers lean unsmoked
    bacon, chopped
1 stick celery, chopped
2 cloves
6 peppercorns
2–3 large sprigs thyme
1 bay leaf
1 dessertspoon plain flour
500ml (18fl oz) stock, made
    either from the deer bones
    or from beef
1 dessertspoon redcurrant jelly
100ml (3½fl oz) red wine
salt

Vegetables

Cornish Potato Cakes

Floury maincrop potatoes are necessary for these tasty cakes.

Peel the potatoes and crumble them into small pieces. Mix with the other ingredients to make a smooth, slightly sticky paste. Don't overwork it. Roll the paste out on a well-floured work surface to a thickness of 1cm (½in). Cut into squares. Bake at 200°C, 400°F, Gas mark 6 for 10–15 minutes until browned and crisp. Eat immediately.

MAKES APPROXIMATELY 18 CAKES

2–3 floury potatoes, total weight 500g (1lb 2oz), boiled in the skins and allowed to cool (but they must not be chilled)
60g (2oz) shredded beef suet
60g (2oz) plain flour, plus extra for dusting
1 teaspoon baking powder
generous pinch of salt

Franklin's Potatoes

Based on a dish from the 1920s, this could be seen as an English type of gratin. It needs waxy potatoes – the new potatoes grown in south Cornwall are perfect. Serve with roast chicken or game as a change from roast potatoes.

Put the milk in a pan with the shallots and cloves and heat to boiling point. Turn off the heat and leave to infuse for at least 30 minutes. Then strain the milk into a clean pan and add the breadcrumbs. Heat gently for few minutes, stirring, until you have a smooth bread sauce. Season rather highly with salt, pepper and spices and add the cream if desired.

Scrub and scrape the potatoes if the skins are easy to remove – otherwise leave them and peel after boiling. Leave the potatoes whole. Cover with cold water, bring to the boil and cook for 10–15 minutes: they should be half-cooked. Drain and leave until cool enough to handle. Remove any patches of skin and slice into rounds about as thick as a pound coin.

Thin the bread sauce, which will have thickened up, with a little extra milk and then use a little sauce to cover the base of the dish. Add a layer of potato slices and continue layering sauce and potatoes until used up, finishing with potatoes. Sprinkle the extra breadcrumbs over the top. Bake at 190°C, 375°F, Gas mark 5 for about an hour.

SERVES 6–8

500ml (18fl oz) milk
2 shallots, peeled and cut
   in quarters
8 whole cloves
60g (2oz) fine white breadcrumbs,
   plus 30g (1oz) or so for
   finishing the dish
salt and pepper
a little ground mace
a pinch of chilli powder
1–2 tablespoons single cream
   (optional)
900g (2lb) medium new potatoes
butter for greasing

You will need a 1.7 litre (3 pint)
soufflé dish or similar

Devonshire Stew

Recorded by Florence White in the 1920s, this is not a stew at all, but more like bubble-and-squeak. Good with ham, bacon or eggs.

Boil the potatoes, whole and unpeeled, until they are almost done. Peel the onions but leave whole, and boil them until tender. Boil the cabbage briefly and press it in a colander with a plate on top to squeeze out as much water as possible.

When the potatoes are cool enough to handle, peel them and cut into long narrow chip shapes. Shred the onion and cabbage. Mix all together and season.

Heat the dripping or butter in a large frying pan and add the vegetables, stirring until the mixture is nicely browned (you may need to do this in two batches). Serve very hot.

SERVES 4

500g (about 1lb) medium
   potatoes, not too floury
   (Desirée work well)
2 medium onions
250g (9oz) cabbage, cut in
   2–3 wedges
1 teaspoon salt and plenty
   of black pepper
beef dripping or butter

Tiesen Nionod

A Welsh dish similar to a gratin, and good with a roast of Welsh lamb.

Butter the inside of a baking dish or deep cake tin. Arrange a layer of potato slices over the base, then add a layer of onions, more potatoes, and so on until all the vegetables are used. Season the layers with salt and pepper, dot with butter and finish with potato. Cover with foil, pressing the vegetables down well, and bake at 180°C, 350°F, Gas mark 4. The cake will cook in about an hour in a hot oven, or 1½ hours in a more moderate one.

A small joint of lamb can be cooked on top of the cake, in which case reduce the amount of butter to about 25g (1oz) and add a little stock.

SERVES 4

900g (2lb) potatoes, preferably a waxy variety such as Desirée, peeled and thinly sliced
400g (14oz) onions, chopped
salt and pepper
80–100g (3–3½oz) butter, plus extra for greasing

Kailkenny

This is a dish of potato and cabbage mixed together in the same manner as Irish colcannon (*kail* or *kale* being a general Scottish word for cabbage). Did the idea spread to Scotland under Irish influence, or was it just a logical response to the ready availability of the ingredients? It is a particularly good version that F. Marian McNeill, a Scottish food and cookery author writing in the early 20th century, attributed to Aberdeenshire and north-eastern Scotland.

Peel the potatoes, cut in chunks and put them on to boil. Wash and trim the cabbage as necessary, then shred finely. Cook gently with a minimum amount of water for about 10 minutes (use a saucepan with a tightly fitting lid and check to make sure it doesn't catch).

When the potatoes are cooked, drain off all but about 2 tablespoons water and mash them. Add the drained cabbage and cream, and mash again. Season to taste.

SERVES 4

2–3 large potatoes (a good
  mashing variety)
about ½ medium cabbage, such
  as January King or Savoy
2–3 tablespoons thick cream
salt and pepper

Champ

Irish comfort food. The standard version uses spring onions but you could use chives instead. Serve with boiled bacon, sliced off the piece, and boiled cabbage.

Peel the potatoes, cut in chunks and boil until tender. Drain, season with salt and pepper and mash with a little of the buttermilk. Chop the greenery into short lengths, add to the buttermilk and warm until almost boiling. Beat the mixture into the mashed potato. Serve very hot in individual portions, each portion shaped into a mound with a hollow, adding a piece of butter in the middle of each.

SERVES 2

500–600g (about 1–1¼lb) potatoes
salt and pepper
100ml (3½fl oz) buttermilk
handful of chives or 6 spring onions
butter to serve

Jugged Peas

To go with all that lovely lamb available from National Trust farms, this is good even for end-of-season, slightly-past-their-best peas. The herbs transform the dish into something to suit 21st-century tastes.

Put the peas, butter, sugar, salt, water and the sprigs of mint in a small casserole or a pudding basin that will hold them comfortably. Cover with a lid or some foil and place the arrangement in a saucepan of water. Bring this to a gentle boil and simmer for 30 minutes. At the end of this time, the peas should be tender and well flavoured. If a more punchy flavour is desired, chop the coriander, mint leaves and chilli finely and stir in just before serving.

SERVES 4

1kg (2¼lb) peas in the pod,
   or 250g (9oz) shelled peas
30g (1oz) butter
1 teaspoon granulated sugar
pinch of salt
1–2 tablespoons water
2 sprigs mint
to finish (optional): 10 sprigs
   fresh coriander, 12 mint leaves
   and a green chilli, de-seeded

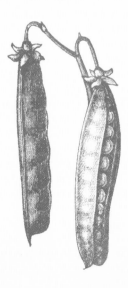

Souffléed Green Pea Pancakes

The Scots seem to have taken to fresh green peas with enthusiasm, as a vegetable or added to broths (and at one point, as a field crop grown for canning). The idea of a soufflé based on fresh peas occurs as both a *haute cuisine* version in *The Cookery Book of Lady Clark of Tillypronie* (1909), and in a more homely version in the *Scottish Women's Rural Institutes Cookery Book* (1952). This takes the idea a step further.

The crowdie sauce is better made a little in advance to allow the flavours to develop. Mix all ingredients together to give a smooth sauce, tasting until you feel a pleasant balance of flavours has been achieved. Chill until needed.

To make the pancakes, put the peas in a pan, add a pinch of salt and a little boiling water – no more than halfway up to the top of the peas. Bring to the boil over high heat, then turn down and cook, uncovered, until the peas are very tender and almost all the water has evaporated. Watch to see that they don't boil dry.

When the peas are cooked, tip them into the goblet of a blender and purée. Tip into a bowl and stir in the butter and Parmesan. Let it cool for 10 minutes, then add the egg yolks. Whisk the egg whites to the soft peak stage and fold into the pea mixture.

Heat a large heavy frying pan and add a little oil – just enough to grease the base. Drop generous tablespoons of mixture into the pan (you will have to cook the pancakes in batches) and fry gently. The bases of the little cakes will brown gently and set. Run a spatula underneath to flip the cakes over and cook lightly on the other side. Keep warm until all the pancakes are cooked, then serve immediately with the sauce.

MAKES ABOUT A DOZEN LITTLE PANCAKES, ENOUGH FOR 3–4 PEOPLE AS A STARTER

200g (7oz) green peas (frozen ones are fine)
pinch of salt
about 15g (½oz) butter
2–3 tablespoons finely grated Parmesan cheese
2 eggs, separated
a little oil for frying (sunflower or other neutral-flavoured vegetable oil)

FOR THE CROWDIE SAUCE
about 150g (5oz) crowdie (a soft creamy cheese traditional to Scotland)
1–2 tablespoons milk
1 tablespoon finely chopped fresh mint
a little grated lemon zest and juice

Stewed Red Cabbage

A good accompaniment to sausages or a nice piece of roast pork. this version is based on a 19th-century recipe from Suffolk.

Cut the cabbage in quarters, remove the stem and slice the leaves thinly. Put the ham and butter in a casserole, and put the cabbage on top. Add the sugar, vinegar and stock. Cook in a low oven 140°C, 275°F, Gas mark 1 for about 2½ hours. Watch it doesn't dry out. Taste and adjust the seasoning, adding salt if necessary and a little more sugar if desired. Grind a little pepper and allspice over just before serving.

SERVES 4–6

1 small red cabbage
100g (3½oz) ham in one piece
20g (¾oz) butter
1–2 tablespoons
    muscovado sugar
75ml (2½fl oz) malt vinegar
200ml (7fl oz) meat stock
    (broth from cooking bacon or
    ham is fine, as long as it's not
    too salty)
pepper and allspice

Parsnip Fritters

Root vegetables – carrots, parsnips, and beetroot – have long been a feature of the East Anglian landscape (see the following page for more information about farmhouse produce from this region). This is an adaptation of a 19th-century method for cooking parsnips.

Boil the parsnips until soft, drain and mash. Stir in the flour. Season with a little salt and a generous grind of pepper. Beat the egg white to soft peak stage and stir into the mixture. Heat the oil or fat in a deep fryer and drop teaspoons of the parsnip mixture into it. Cook for 3–4 minutes until golden brown and slightly puffed. Drain on kitchen paper, sprinkle with salt and serve alongside grilled steak.

SERVES 4

400g (14oz) parsnips, peeled
  and cut into chunks
30g (1oz) plain flour
salt and pepper
1 egg white
oil or fat for deep frying

Farmhouse Cookery in East Anglia

East Anglia begins on the banks of the Thames Estuary east of London, in the creeks and tidal marshes of Essex, smoothing into the long, straight coast north of Felixstowe, then curving back into the sands of the Wash. In this northern corner are the Fens, perfectly level black soil drained by a grid of water-filled ditches. If this area resembles the Netherlands, it is partly because the topography is similar but also because the Dutch helped with its drainage. A low ridge divides these from the flat land of east Norfolk and the wetlands of the Broads. South of Cambridge, the countryside rises a little and becomes less stern as it turns into Suffolk, a comfortable region of low rolling hills, pretty villages of half-timbered or pink-washed houses and huge churches.

Wheat grows well here in the relatively warm, dry summers. East Anglia has the lowest average rainfall in the country, but some of the most bitter winter winds, sweeping in across the North Sea from central Europe. The coastline, under constant threat from erosion by the sea, includes salt marshes – which support plants such as samphire and sea lavender (which produces a distinctive pale yellow-green honey) – shingle and sand, tidal inlets and the Broads. Wild-fowling and fishing were traditional pursuits of the Broads and Fens, and landowners shot game, particularly partridges, which fed on the grain crops. In Norfolk, some of the Breckland survives as a distinctive area of sandy heath; the rest has been forested or become arable farmland with hedge-like boundaries of twisted pines. The vast commercial rabbit warrens, which once provided income for this area, have gone in all except name, as places such as Thetford Warren, Santon Warren and Wangford Warren remind us. Further south, heathland also featured on the coast of Suffolk in an area known as the Sandlings which, together with the Essex marshes, were important for grazing livestock.

The area is now thought of in terms of grain and vegetables, but this is not exclusively the case and never has been. True, grain has always been important, and East Anglian arable farms were often large and wealthy. But the obsession with monocultures of wheat or barley is a modern one; previously, the local economy had to be more self-sufficient. The traditional cattle breed of the area, Red Polls, were dual-purpose animals, bred for both beef and dairying. No one would consider East Anglia dairy country now, but a delicious, soft cheese was made in the Ely area in the early 20th century (see page 200). Suffolk sheep, with their chocolate-coloured heads and legs, are popular with farmers far beyond the county, and Suffolk also developed characteristic cures for hams and bacon, using black treacle and brown sugar. Rearing poultry, especially geese and turkeys, is a traditional East Anglian pursuit.

Vegetables and fruit also play their part in the rural landscape. They include cabbages, root vegetables (such as the typical East Anglian recipe on the previous page), asparagus and apples, plums and soft fruit, which are important as there are two major jam-making companies in the area. A more unusual crop is mustard, although less is grown nowadays. Local baking traditions include little rusks known as Norfolk knobs, and dumplings, sometimes credited to Norfolk, sometimes to Suffolk, made from plain yeasted bread dough and cooked in boiling water.

Wicken Fen, Cambridgeshire.

Mushrooms in Cream

The Derbyshire childhood of the children's author Alison Uttley is beautifully evoked in her book *Recipes From an Old Farmhouse*, in which she describes cooking mushrooms in saucers of cream for breakfast or tea. Juicy, delicately flavoured field mushrooms are best. Cultivated mushrooms need a little help.

Wipe the mushrooms and trim the stems close to the caps. Place in the dish cap down. Sprinkle with salt and pepper and scatter the herbs and garlic over. Pour the cream over. Bake, uncovered, in a hot oven at 220°C, 425°F, Gas mark 7 for 20 minutes, or until the mushrooms are cooked. Baste the mushrooms with the cream halfway through cooking.

Serve on toast, or leave in the cooking dish and mop up the juices with fresh bread.

SERVES 1

6–8 button mushrooms
salt and pepper
1 tablespoon chopped
    fresh parsley
1–2 sprigs thyme, chopped
1 small garlic clove, crushed
75ml (3fl oz) single cream

You will need a small, shallow ovenproof dish that will just hold the mushrooms

Pickled Red Cabbage

In the Lake District, this pickle is always served with tatie pot (see page 81).

Quarter the cabbage and remove the stem. Shred the leaves, sprinkle with salt and leave to stand overnight. The next day, rinse off the salt and drain thoroughly. Boil the vinegar, sugar and spice together for 10 minutes, then allow to cool a little. Pack the cabbage in warmed, wide-mouthed jars and strain the vinegar mixture over. Tie down and leave for a week before using.

SERVES 4

1 medium red cabbage,
    outer leaves removed
salt
600ml (1 pint) malt vinegar
1 tablespoon granulated sugar
1 tablespoon pickling spice

Onions with Cream Sauce and Wensleydale Cheese

An onion could provide a meal for a countryman or woman – a boiled or baked onion was a favourite with one of my aunts, as in this recipe using Yorkshire's best-known cheese.

Peel the onions but leave them whole. Simmer gently in water until tender (this depends on size, but test after 30 minutes).

To make the sauce, melt the butter and add the flour to make a roux. Gradually blend in the milk and stir constantly until the sauce thickens. Allow it to cook gently on the lowest possible heat for 10–15 minutes. Add the cream, taste and add the seasonings. Split each onion in half and arrange in a shallow ovenproof dish. Pour over the sauce, scatter the cheese on top and flash under a hot grill to melt the cheese.

SERVES 4

4 large, mild onions
30g (1oz) butter
2 tablespoons plain flour
250ml (9fl oz) milk
90ml (3fl oz) double cream
salt, pepper and a little nutmeg
60g (2oz) Wensleydale
   cheese, grated

Hot Puddings

Apple Pancakes with Cider Sauce

A pudding influenced by the cider and apple tradition of the south-west of England. Cider-makers sometimes give their products extra flavour by storing them in barrels formerly used for fortified wine or spirits. I use a Devon cider which has been kept in a rum barrel.

Put the apples in a saucepan with 1 tablespoon water and cook very gently until soft.

Mix the flour and salt with the eggs, then beat in the rum and milk to make a smooth batter. Use this to make 12 thin pancakes.

Spread each pancake with a little of the apple purée, roll up and arrange on a heatproof dish. Put in a low oven 170°C, 325°F, Gas mark 3 for 5–10 minutes to warm and crisp a little on the edges.

Melt the butter in a pan and stir in the sugar. Add the cider, bring to the boil and cook rapidly until the mixture has reduced by at least half and is slightly syrupy. Serve hot with the pancakes.

SERVES 6

2–3 large, well-flavoured
   apples, peeled and sliced
100g (3½oz) plain flour
pinch of salt
2 eggs
1 tablespoon rum
250ml (9fl oz) milk
50g (1¾oz) butter, plus extra
   for frying the pancakes
50g (1¾oz) demerara sugar
300ml (½ pint) cider

Potato and Apple Cake

A variation on apple pie, from an Irish recipe given by Florence White. Use Bramley apples grown in Armagh to give a taste of Ulster.

Boil the potatoes until tender. Mash well and allow to cool a little. Put the flour and a little salt in a bowl and grate in the dripping or butter. Mix well and add the potato and the egg yolk to make a soft dough; add a little milk if it seems on the dry side but try not to overmix. Divide into 3 portions, one slightly bigger; roll this one out and use to line the pie dish. Cover the base with half the apples and scatter in half the sugar. Roll out a second portion of dough and put over the apples; scatter the remaining apples on top of this and add the rest of the sugar. Roll out the third portion of dough and use it to cover the pie, sealing the edges. Glaze with the beaten egg.

Bake at 200°C, 400°F, Gas mark 6 for 20 minutes, then turn the heat down to 180°C, 350°F, Gas mark 4 and continue to cook for 20–25 minutes, or until the pastry is golden-brown in patches.

This is best eaten hot, straight from the oven as the pastry becomes very solid when cold, although it can be reheated.

SERVES 8

FOR THE PASTRY
2 large potatoes, peeled and
   cut into chunks
250g (9oz) plain flour
salt
80g (3oz) beef dripping or butter
1 egg yolk, plus 1 whole egg,
   beaten, to glaze
60ml (2fl oz) milk (optional)

FOR THE FILLING
1kg (2¼lb) apples, peeled,
   cored and sliced
175g (6oz) demerara sugar

You will need a deep pie dish
20cm (8in) in diameter

Pear Tarts

The rich dough made for Sally Lunns can be used in the same way as rich yeast doughs sometimes are in France, as a base for tarts.

Flour your hands and the work surface and divide the dough into 8 pieces. Shape each piece into a thin disc 12–15cm (5–6in) in diameter. Divide the pears between the dough circles.

Dot with butter and sprinkle with a little sugar. Bake at 200°C, 400°F, Gas mark 6 for 10 minutes, then turn the heat down to 180°C, 350°F, Gas mark 4 and cook for another 5 minutes, until the dough is crisp and golden. Serve warm, with cream if desired.

MAKES 8

plain flour for dusting
1 quantity Sally Lunn dough
   (see page 210), after rising
4 large ripe Conference pears,
   peeled, cored, quartered and
   thinly sliced
50g (1¾oz) butter
brown sugar for sprinkling

Caramelised Baked Pumpkin

Mr Upton began gardening at Slindon Estate in West Sussex in the 1950s. As he couldn't interest anyone in the traditional apple varieties growing there, he began cultivating pumpkins and squashes instead. This recipe works well with any variety.

Cut the pumpkin into rough cubes. Melt the butter in a shallow ovenproof dish. Add the pumpkin and turn it in the butter so that it is well coated. Sprinkle with salt, pepper and the sugar. Bake at 240°C, 475°F, Gas mark 9 for 15 minutes, then reduce the heat to 220°C, 425°F, Gas mark 7 for a further 10 minutes, or until the pumpkin is tender. Serve immediately.

SERVES 4–6

1kg (2¼lb) pumpkin, peeled, deseeded and stringy centre removed
30g (1oz) butter
salt and freshly ground black pepper
2 tablespoons demerara sugar

Cherry Bumpers

A sort of cherry turnover, traditional to Buckinghamshire, where cherries were once an important crop.

Roll out the pastry fairly thinly and cut out six 10–12cm (4–5in) circles.

Mix the almonds with 2 tablespoons of caster sugar and work a drop of almond essence through the mixture with your fingers. Put a little of this almond mixture in the centre of each pastry circle, then divide the cherries between them. Brush round the edge of each piece with a little cold water and crimp the edges firmly to enclose the filling. Brush the top of each little parcel with water and then sprinkle with caster sugar.

Place on a greased baking tray and bake at 200°C, 400°F, Gas mark 6 for 12–15 minutes. Eat warm – but be careful when they are fresh from the oven as the cherries become very hot – or cold.

MAKES 6

1 quantity shortcrust pastry
   made with butter and lard
   mixed (see page 13)
1 tablespoon ground almonds
caster sugar
1 drop bitter almond essence
250g (9oz) fresh cherries, stoned

Sutton Wakes Pudding

This Peak District recipe is like a hot version of summer pudding. A 'wake' was originally a vigil or watch observed to honour the local parish's patron saint. From an overnight vigil the 'wake' eventually became a celebration or fair, sometimes lasting as long as a week.

Mix the flour and breadcrumbs together. Using the coarse side of a grater, grate the cold butter into the mixture and distribute as evenly as possible. Add enough cold water, a tablespoon at a time, to make a firm dough. Roll the dough out and use it to line the prepared basin, reserving a quarter to make a lid. Add the fruit in layers, scattering sugar in between. Roll the remaining pastry into a circle, dampen the edges and place it over the filling, sealing well. Trim off any excess, cover with a double layer of foil and tie on firmly with string, making a loop over the top as a handle. Place in a large pan and add boiling water to come halfway up the sides of the basin. Steam for 2 hours. Serve hot with cold thick cream.

You can try unmoulding this pudding, but use a deep dish as lots of juice will flow out of it; be prepared for it to collapse. It's safer to serve it straight from the bowl.

SERVES 4–6

150g (5oz) self-raising flour

100g (3½oz) fine white breadcrumbs

100g (3½oz) salted butter, well chilled

750g (1lb 10oz) mixed soft fruit, such as blackcurrants, strawberries, raspberries, redcurrants, gooseberries or rhubarb

80g (3oz) caster sugar

You will need a 1.2 litre (2 pint) pudding basin greased with a little softened butter and sprinkled with a little demerara sugar

Devon Whitepot

Originally a whitepot was sausage-like, a distant relative of the hog's puddings still sold in the south-west of England. By the 18th century it was a recipe for a rich, creamy bread and butter pudding, well worth making. Use really good-quality raisins for the traditional Devonshire recipe (see the following page for more about farmhouse produce from Devon).

Mix the spices and a little of the sugar and toss the butter cubes in it. Then build up the pudding in the dish, starting with a layer of bread. Scatter half the butter cubes, dates, raisins and citron peel over, add another layer of bread, the rest of the butter and fruit, and finish with a neatly arranged layer of bread.

Beat the egg yolks, cream and the rest of the sugar together, and pour over the pudding; the bread should absorb the mixture, although you may have to press it down a little.

Bake at 170°C, 325°F, Gas mark 3 for 30–40 minutes, until the custard is just set and the top golden brown. Serve hot.

SERVES 4–6

½ teaspoon ground ginger
½ teaspoon ground cinnamon
60g (2oz) caster sugar
30g (1oz) butter, cut into small dice, plus extra for greasing
100g (3½oz) slightly stale white bread, crusts removed, cut in very thin slices
60g (2oz) dates, stoned and sliced lengthways
60g (2oz) raisins, stoned if necessary
30g (1oz) candied citron peel, thinly sliced
6 egg yolks, beaten
500ml (18fl oz) single cream

You will need a deep baking dish, such as a 15cm (6in) diameter soufflé dish, buttered well

Farmhouse Cookery in Devon

After the tough, windswept plateau of Cornwall, south Devon feels like a duvet. Past the Tamar Valley, green with moss and ivy-hung trees, the countryside is rounded and soft. The wind is less fierce than in Cornwall. The buildings follow the soft shapes of the cob and thatch tradition, and are tucked away in the folds of deep valleys, known as combes, to which access is down steep narrow lanes outlined by high, parallel banks, hung with hartstongue ferns. Sometimes the walls that wind along the village lanes are capped with thatch as well. Not all of Devon is so gentle. The hills rise in ridges, gradually losing their enclosed feeling until they meet Dartmoor, a horizon of pointed granite tors which reach heights of over 400m (1,300ft) and catch the snow in winter. Dartmoor must always have been difficult to farm and is now marginal to agriculture, although prehistoric field systems hidden beneath the bracken, heather and scrub show that people have tried to cultivate it. From here the land is sparsely populated, rising north to Exmoor, a slab of peat-capped red sandstone emerging steeply out of the sea. Both environments are suitable only for rough grazing and game such as red deer. North Devon feels somewhat like a continuation of Cornwall. The vegetation may be softer, a little less harassed by the wind and salt, but rain, in huge quantities, influences this landscape, as the deep gorges, and occasional dramatic floods, such as that at Lynmouth in the 1950s, demonstrate.

The varied landscape, from the soft climate of the sheltered south coast to the grass and heather tops of Exmoor, has given rise to two breeds of cattle, both a deep rich red. North Devons are hairy and tough beef cattle originally developed for the rough grazing of Exmoor. The South Devons, influenced by the Channel Islands, are dairy cattle, which contribute to the clotted cream and butter tradition so essential to perceptions of the county. Cheese, historically, was of less importance, although both Cheddar-style cheese and some continentally influenced cheeses are now made here.

The native sheep breed is the hardy Dartmoor. Both sheep and cattle produce good meat; some of it is grazed on National Trust land adjacent to the Salcombe Estuary. Pigs also become more important. Devon cures for ham are usually brine based rather than dry salt. 'You try and stop it turning into brine', a Devon farmer's wife said to me, in acknowledgement of the humid climate.

The soft climate is good for potatoes and other vegetables, although few distinctive recipes appear to exist for them. Soft fruit such as strawberries also do well; after all, one has to have something to eat with the clotted cream. The south-western apple and cider tradition is very strong. Apples were used in some meat dishes recorded in the first half of the 20th century, such as pies of mutton, apples and onions. These seem to have vanished, and possibly needed the slow heat of a brick bread oven to make them really well. The little bread rolls made in Cornwall under the name of splits were recorded in Devon as chudleighs, but seem to have been overtaken by scones as a base for strawberry jam and clotted cream. Clotted cream is also eaten with good Dartmoor heather honey or with golden syrup, a combination known as 'thunder and lightning'. As in Cornwall, cream and butter are also used as an enriching ingredient for pies, although the habit of putting everything in pastry is less pronounced.

Exe Valley in Devon.

Bakewell Pudding

This version was recorded by the children's author Alison Uttley, a Derbyshire native who grew up not far from Bakewell. It's a lovely, rich dish for special occasions.

Roll out the pastry thinly and use it to line the dish, trimming the edges neatly. Spread a generous layer of jam over the base. Mix together the egg yolks, butter, sugar, almonds and the almond essence. Beat the whites to a froth and stir in.

Bake at 180°C, 350°F, Gas mark 4 for about 40 minutes. Serve tepid.

SERVES 6

250g (9oz) puff pastry
  (ready-made pastry is fine)
100–150g (3½–5oz) raspberry jam
4 egg yolks
100g (3½oz) butter, melted
100g (3½oz) caster sugar
100g (3½oz) ground almonds
1 drop bitter almond essence
2 egg whites

You will need a deep oval dish of the type used for baking rice puddings – mine holds 850ml (1½ pints)

Anne Horne's Butter Tart

Also known as Border tart, there are numerous variations of this north-eastern favourite. All are very sweet – treats for people who worked long days in the cold.

Roll out the pastry and use it to line the flan dish. Mix all the other ingredients together and pour into the case. Bake at 200°C, 400°F, Gas mark 6 for 30–40 minutes. Serve warm with whipped cream.

1 quantity shortcrust pastry
  (see page 13)
80g (3oz) butter, melted
300g (10oz) currants or
  mixed fruit
300g (10oz) demerara sugar
3 eggs
2–3 drops vanilla essence

You will need a 23cm (9in)
round flan dish

Treacle Custard Tart

This is a sweet but addictive dessert, which Florence White recorded as a dish from East Anglia.

Roll out the pastry and use it to line the tart tin. Cover the pastry with greaseproof paper, fill with dried beans and bake blind for 15 minutes at 180°C, 350°F, Gas mark 4. Remove the paper and beans and return to the oven for another 5 minutes.

Put the syrup and butter in a pan over a gentle heat. When the butter has melted, remove from the heat and add the lemon juice and zest, then the eggs, mixing well. Pour into the pastry case and bake at 150°C, 300°F, Gas mark 2 for 30–35 minutes, until just set in the middle. Serve cool but not chilled.

1 quantity shortcrust pastry made with butter (see page 13)
200g (7oz) golden syrup
30g (1oz) butter
grated zest and juice of 1 lemon
2 eggs, beaten

You will need an 18–20cm (7–8in) round tart tin

Treacle Tart

This actually uses golden syrup, but was always known as treacle tart. This Yorkshire recipe is a more elaborate version than the simple syrup-and-breadcrumb concoctions I knew as a child.

Roll out the pastry and line the tin. Add the currants, sultanas and peel. Mix together all the other ingredients and spoon over the top, levelling neatly. Bake at 200°C, 400°F, Gas mark 6 for 20 minutes, then lower the temperature to 180°C, 350°F, Gas mark 4 for a further 10 minutes. Serve warm with cream or custard.

SERVES 4–6

½ quantity shortcrust pastry made with butter and lard mixed (see page 13)
50g (1¾oz) currants
50g (1¾oz) sultanas
50g (1¾oz) mixed candied peel, chopped
60g (2oz) brown breadcrumbs
1 apple, peeled and grated
pinch of ground ginger
pinch of mixed spice
2 generous tablespoons golden syrup, warmed
grated zest and juice of 1 lemon

You will need an 18cm (7in) round pie tin

Cumberland Clipping Time Pudding

Christine Edmund, who sent this recipe from the Lake District, says that this was one of the special dishes provided on sheep-clipping day when all the neighbours came to help. The quantities given will serve about 8 people (unless they've been clipping sheep, in which case it might not stretch as far).

Pour some boiling water over the rice to blanch it, then drain. Put in a large pan with the milk, salt, sugar and cinnamon and simmer very gently, stirring occasionally, until the rice is tender, about 40 minutes. Transfer to an ovenproof dish and stir in the butter, dried fruit and beaten egg. Bake at 190°C, 375°F, Gas mark 5 for 20 minutes. Serve warm.

SERVES 8

150g (5½oz) pudding rice
1.5 litres (2¼ pints) milk
pinch of salt
80g (3oz) sugar
½ teaspoon cinnamon
60g (2oz) butter
100g (3½oz) currants
100g (3½oz) raisins or sultanas
1 egg, beaten

Snowdon Pudding

A recipe that appears in all books on Welsh cookery. Its connection to Wales is that in the 19th century it was served in a hotel at the foot of Mount Snowdon.

Divide the raisins but don't cut them completely in two. Use them to make a pattern round the inside of the pudding basin, sticking them cut side to the butter. Mix the dry ingredients and marmalade. Beat the eggs well and stir in. Put the mixture in the basin, cover with foil or greaseproof paper, tie with string, and lower into a pan of boiling water. Boil for 1¼ hours.

Serve with Sherry or Madeira Sauce (below).

SERVES 6–8

30g (1oz) butter
80g (3oz) good-quality raisins
250g (9oz) shredded suet
250g (9oz) fine white breadcrumbs
40g (1½oz) rice flour or cornflour
pinch of salt
150g (5oz) soft light brown sugar
150g (5oz) lemon marmalade
   (orange marmalade can be
   used instead)
6 eggs
grated zest of 2 lemons

You will need a 1.2 litre (2 pint)
pudding basin, lavishly buttered

Sherry or Madeira Sauce

A sauce to accompany Snowdon Pudding (above).

Simmer the lemon zest and sugar in the water for 10 minutes. Remove and discard the zest. Knead the butter and flour together and add, in small pieces, to the lemon-flavoured syrup. Heat gently to thicken and add the sherry or Madeira.

zest of ½ lemon, removed in thin
   pieces with a potato peeler
30g (1oz) granulated sugar
150ml (¼ pint) water
2 teaspoons plain flour
50g (1oz) butter
75ml (2½fl oz) sherry or Madeira

Gingerbread Crumble

The short-textured zesty gingerbread of the style associated with Grasmere (see page 256) also makes an excellent crumble-type pudding, such as this one from the Lake District.

Put the raspberries in a baking dish. Rub the butter into the flour, then stir in the remaining ingredients. Cover the fruit with this mixture (don't press it down). Bake at 180°C, 350°F, Gas mark 4 for 30 minutes. Serve tepid with cream.

SERVES 6

500g (about 1lb) fresh
    raspberries
150g (5oz) butter
250g (9oz) self-raising flour
120g (4oz) soft light brown sugar
1 teaspoon ground ginger
½ teaspoon grated lemon zest

Cold Puddings

Clotted Cream and Blackberry Ripple Ice

Cook the blackberries gently until they have yielded all their juice. Rub through a sieve, discarding the pulp. Measure 150ml (¼ pint) of juice, mix in the sugar and bring to the boil. Allow to cool.

For the custard, put the milk and half the sugar in a pan and heat to almost boiling. Beat the egg yolks with the remaining sugar until the mixture is pale and holds its shape when a ribbon of mix is trailed across the surface. Pour the hot milk in a steady stream onto the egg and sugar mixture, beating steadily. Place the bowl over a pan of simmering water and allow to thicken. Stir frequently. When the mixture coats the back of a wooden spoon and holds a horizontal line drawn across the spoon, it is thick enough. Remove the bowl and plunge the base into cold water to stop it cooking further. Then stir in the clotted cream. Allow to cool, stirring occasionally, then chill.

To freeze in an electric ice cream machine, churn the cream mix for 10 minutes (no longer, or it will become buttery), then scrape it into a plastic freezer box. Add the blackberry and sugar mixture and marble it through the semi-frozen ice cream. Transfer to the freezer for an hour.

Without a machine, put the cream mix in a freezer box, cover and put in the freezer. After an hour, scrape the edge to the centre of the mixture and beat for a few seconds with an electric hand beater to form a uniform slush. Return to the freezer. Repeat the process after another hour. Marble the blackberry mixture through. Allow to freeze until set.

Give the ice about 15 minutes to soften before serving if it has been frozen solid.

FOR THE BLACKBERRY RIPPLE
500g (1lb 2oz) blackberries
150g (5oz) sugar

FOR THE CUSTARD
375ml (13fl oz) milk
120g (4oz) granulated sugar
5 egg yolks
125ml (4fl oz) clotted cream

Mrs Palmer's Russian Cream

Gillian Palmer, from Lanteglos near Fowey, Cornwall, remarks that this recipe was 'a great favourite with the teams of men who followed the threshing machines around the farms' in the early 20th century. Similar dishes have been made in Britain since at least the 18th century, and don't seem to have much to do with Russia. It's well worth experimenting with different flavourings. Try a little lemon zest or vanilla essence.

Put the milk into a saucepan. Add the egg yolks, sugar, flavouring if used, and sprinkle the gelatine over. Stir well to break up the egg yolks and distribute the gelatine well, and put over a low heat. Meanwhile, whisk the egg whites to a stiff foam.

Increase the heat and bring just to the boil, stirring all the time (don't worry if it shows signs of curdling). Remove from the heat and stir the beaten egg whites through the mixture. Turn into a bowl and leave overnight in a cool place.

To serve, put a plate over the bowl, invert and shake gently. The pudding should slide out, and will have a clear jelly layer and a foamy layer. Serve with clotted cream.

SERVES 6

500ml (18fl oz) full-fat milk
2 eggs, separated
100g (3½oz) caster sugar
a few drops vanilla essence
    or a little grated lemon zest
1 sachet powdered gelatine

Raspberry Cream

A recipe based on one from a cookery manuscript dated 1847, belonging to the National Trust. This is especially nice made with rich cream from the west country (for more on traditional Cornish ingredients, see the following page).

Serve in glasses, one per person, and set aside a few of the nicest raspberries for a garnish.

Rub the rest of the berries through a sieve, discarding the pips. Mix the raspberry purée with the sugar and brandy; put about a tablespoon of this into the bottom of each glass. Add the cream to the remainder and beat until stiff. Spoon into the glasses on top of the purée. Decorate with mint sprigs and the whole raspberries. Chill.

SERVES 4–6

350g (12oz) raspberries
70g (2½oz) caster sugar
2 tablespoons brandy
250ml (9fl oz) double cream
mint sprigs

Farmhouse Cookery in Cornwall

Cornwall may be Britain's southernmost county, but that doesn't mean the climate is easy. 'We get salt gales here which kill the nettles,' says Rod Brake, a tenant on National Trust land near Porth Mawgan. Mr Brake's farm is on a cliff-top and in January that means horizontal rain mixed with salt spray from the sea pounding the rocks below. It's not especially cold, but it's tough. The wind and the rain it sweeps in off hundreds of miles of uninterrupted ocean is a force to be reckoned with for much of the year.

By the time most visitors get there, in summer, the fields have become soft and green, the sea has calmed down, and they wonder why hedges are planted on top of granite walls, which obscure the view and are unforgiving for the careless or inattentive driver. They are windbreaks, offering a little protection to both man and beast. There aren't many trees, and the ones that are there lean away from the west at 45 degree angles, even on the south coast.

On three sides Cornwall rises out of the sea, mostly as steep cliffs. On top the land is surprisingly level. In the south-western part of the county the cliffs are softened in places by the Fowey and Carrick Roads, hung with trees and many-coloured little towns like a child's paintbox. Otherwise, the traditional architecture has a stern, small-windowed simplicity which reflects the hard building stone and the need to exclude wind and rain. Roofs are slate, not thatch. On the fourth side the county shares a boundary with Devon, marked for much of its length by the River Tamar. It is a mistake to think of Cornwall as a purely agricultural landscape; it has been mined for tin in the south-west, for china clay in the St Austell area and for smooth charcoal-grey slate at Delabole.

How does this particular combination of rain and wind, soil and grass, of scattered farms and little semi-industrial mining communities and fishing towns express itself in food? To the summer tourist, the most obvious items are pasties, clotted cream and fish (see previous page for a typical Cornish recipe). The climate is not especially conducive to growing corn, and historically barley bread may have been as important as wheat. Possibly locally grown wheat flour was more suitable for pastry; there are certainly numerous traditional pastry dishes in Cornish cookery books, and Cornish saffron cake, really a type of fruit bread, has a long history. A vegetable and herb tradition is apparent in some of the fillings cited for pasties and pies: leeks, parsley and the more general catch-all of 'herbs'. The relatively mild temperatures and good soils of the south-westernmost part of the county produce excellent early potatoes and other vegetables. While most fields are pretty much square, on the north coast traces of medieval strip systems have been fossilised in patterns of grass and hedgerow – these are known as 'stitchfields' and are particularly apparent at Forrabury Stitches above Boscastle, but can also be glimpsed elsewhere.

Grazing sheep and cattle for meat production is also very important. Several National Trust tenants use traditional animal breeds in land management schemes, such as Manx Loaghtan sheep or Devon cattle grazed on the cliffs east of the Fowey Estuary. Somehow, magically, this slightly unpromising landscape also produces clotted cream, one of the richest and most unctuous of British dairy produce, for which Cornwall is justly famous. Cheese-making, while never as strong a tradition as in Somerset, has benefited from the creativity of the past few decades and Cornish Yarg has become respected as a new cheese and a local speciality. Finally, the sea itself provided employment for sailors and fishermen and brought sources of food beyond those of just the land, and fish is often combined in the cream and pastry tradition.

Organically reared pigs on Bosigran Farm in Cornwall.

Stewed Pears

A delicious variation on pears in red wine, traditionally made in September, the time of the Barnstaple Fair in Devon.

Put the pears in a pan with the sugar, lemon zest and juice, port, cloves and enough water to cover. Add a drop of cochineal, if you want them to be really pink. Simmer gently for about 20 minutes or until the pears are tender. Cool and decorate with the almonds. Serve chilled with single cream.

SERVES 6

6 medium pears, peeled,
    cored and sliced
350g (12oz) granulated sugar
zest and juice of 1 lemon
100ml (3½fl oz) port
3–4 cloves
about 500ml (18fl oz) water
1 drop cochineal
slivered almonds, toasted

Plums and Cream

Fruit was often simply stewed and served with custard or cream to make simple puddings in the garden of England. This version is good made with purple Early Rivers plums, developed by Thomas Rivers in the 19th century.

Put the plums, sugar, water and the vanilla pod in a pan and cook very gently until the plums are soft. Remove the vanilla pod. At this point, you can either leave the plums whole or make a slightly more complex and elegant dish by coarsely sieving them or putting them through a *mouli-légumes*. If you do this, take a dozen plum stones, break them and add the kernels to the purée. Chill well and serve in glasses with a good spoonful of sour cream or crème fraîche in each.

SERVES 4–6

500g (about 1lb) plums
200g (7oz) sugar
150ml (¼ pint) water
1 vanilla pod, split lengthways
sour cream or crème fraîche
    to serve

Oldbury Gooseberry Pies

These pies are made with a hot-water crust and a hand-raised shell. The recipe and method is local to Oldbury-on-Severn, Gloucestershire, where the pies are still made for summer fêtes and fund-raising events. Traditionally, the edges are nipped up into 21 little points, and the pies themselves full of juice. Make the pies the day before you cook them for the best results.

Put the flour in a bowl. Cut the butter and lard into small dice, make a well in the centre of the flour and place the fat in it. Pour the boiling water over and rapidly mix until you have a warm, malleable dough. Divide into 8 pieces and work with one piece at a time; keep the remainder covered with a cloth, in a warm place. Take the piece of dough, cut away a quarter to make a lid, and roll the rest out into a circle slightly smaller than a saucer. Make the tart cases by turning the edges up by 2cm (¾in) all round, pinching the pastry so that it stands up. Fill with some of the gooseberries and a fairly liberal amount of sugar. Roll the smaller piece of pastry into a circle big enough for a lid, brush with water and use it to cover the berries and sugar, pinching the edges together all round. Repeat with the other pieces of pastry.

Place on baking trays and leave overnight in a cool place for the pastry to set. Bake at 200–220°C, 400–425°F, Gas mark 6–7 for 25–30 minutes. Serve tepid or allow to cool. I've never managed to make them without some juice escaping, but they still taste good.

MAKES 8

500g (1lb 2oz) plain flour
125g (4½oz) butter
125g (4½oz) lard
5 tablespoons boiling water
750g (1lb 10oz) small green
    gooseberries
250–325g (9–11oz)
    demerara sugar

Gooseberries with Elderberry Zabaglione

Most country people grew gooseberries – they were low-maintenance and provided home-grown fruit early in the summer. I don't think gooseberry fool (cooked, crushed berries, custard and whipped cream) can be improved on, but sometimes one might want a change, as in this recipe. Make the purée in advance, while the zabaglione is a last-minute task.

SERVES 4

300g (10oz) gooseberries
4 egg yolks
4 tablespoons granulated sugar
4 tablespoons elderflower cordial
1 tablespoon vodka (optional)

Put the gooseberries in a pan with just enough water to cover the base. Cook gently until soft, then sieve. Chill the purée.

Just before serving, divide the purée between four dishes or glasses. Put the egg yolks and sugar in a bowl and beat with a whisk until pale yellow. Add the cordial and vodka. Put the bowl over a pan of simmering water (don't let it touch the water, or it will curdle) and keep beating until thick and foamy. Divide this between the dishes and serve immediately, perhaps with some little almond biscuits.

Blackberry Jelly

Blackberries grow everywhere in Britain and are used for all sorts of crumbles, pies and puddings.

Rinse the blackberries and put them in a pan with the vanilla pod. Cover tightly and cook gently for a few minutes until they have yielded all their juice. Strain through a jelly bag; retrieve and rinse the vanilla pod for use another day, discard the pulp and measure the juice. Make up to 500ml (18fl oz) with water if the quantity is a little short.

Put the juice in a pan and heat gently until almost boiling. Put 100ml (3½fl oz) juice in a cup or small bowl and add the gelatine, stirring to dissolve the powder. Add the sugar to the remaining juice and continue to stir until this, too, has dissolved. Remove the pan from the heat. Stir in the gelatine mixture. Pour into a serving dish or glasses, or rinse a jelly mould in cold water and pour in the mixture. Allow to set and serve chilled.

750g (1lb 10oz) blackberries
1 vanilla pod
1 sachet powdered gelatine
120g (4oz) granulated sugar

Rhubarb and Ginger Fool

This needs the bright pink early season rhubarb grown in special forcing sheds south of Wakefield in Yorkshire.

Trim off the leaves and bases of the rhubarb stems, wash the stalks and cut into 2cm (¾in) lengths. Place in an ovenproof dish, add the sugar, cover and bake at 170°C, 325°F, Gas mark 3 for 30–40 minutes. Allow to cool.

Whip the cream until thick but not stiff and fold into the rhubarb mixture. Slice the ginger and stir in. Serve chilled.

SERVES 4–6

600g (1¼lb) forced rhubarb
100g (3½oz) light brown sugar
250ml (9fl oz) whipping cream
4–5 pieces of preserved stem ginger, drained of syrup

Damson Sauce

Damson trees were originally planted in the Lyth Valley in the Lake District to provide fruit for use as a dye for cloth. Their blossom has become a feature of the landscape in spring and the fruit is also used locally in many dishes. This damson sauce recipe came from Marion Hayton in Penrith.

Put the damsons, port, cloves, cinnamon and sugar in a pan and bring to the boil. Cover and simmer for 15 minutes then add the jelly and fruit juice. Mix thoroughly and bring back to the boil. Cool and sieve. Excellent served over meringues and whipped cream.

250g (9oz) damsons,
   washed and dried
250ml (9fl oz) port
2 cloves
generous pinch of
   ground cinnamon
30g (1oz) soft brown sugar
3 tablespoons redcurrant jelly
juice of 1 lemon and
   1 orange

Spiced Plum Tart

A Pembrokeshire farmer's wife contributed this recipe to *Farmhouse Fare*, published by the *Farmers Weekly* magazine in 1950.

Mix the flour, icing sugar, cinnamon, spice and salt in a bowl. Rub in the butter and add enough water to make a stiffish dough.

Roll out two-thirds of the pastry and use it to line a pie dish. Add the plums, apples and sugar. Use the remaining pastry to cover and seal the pie. Glaze the pastry with beaten egg or milk. Bake at 200°C, 400°F, Gas mark 6 for 20 minutes, then lower the heat to 180°C, 350°F, Gas mark 4 and cook for another 20–25 minutes. Serve hot or cold.

SERVES 6–8

250g (9oz) plain flour
40g (1½oz) icing sugar
½ teaspoon ground cinnamon
pinch of mixed spice
pinch of salt
125g (4½oz) butter
450g (1lb) plums, halved and stoned
4 small apples, peeled, cored and sliced
200g (7oz) sugar
beaten egg or milk to glaze

Hazelnut Cake

The crunch of the hazelnuts contrasts pleasingly with the raspberries in this light sponge.

Whisk the egg yolks and sugar together until thick and pale. Add the lemon juice. Fold in the groun nuts, then the flour. Whisk the egg whites until they hold a stiff peak. Stir a third of the whites into the hazelnut mixture to slacken it off, then gently fold in the remaining whites. Pour the mixture into the cake tin and bake at 180°C, 350°F, Gas mark 4 for 35–40 minutes. Cool in the tin. When cool, remove from the tin, carefully slice in half horizontally and fill with whipped cream and raspberries.

3 large eggs, separated
175g (6oz) caster sugar
juice of ½ a lemon
60g (2oz) hazelnuts, skin
  on, finely ground
30g (1oz) plain flour, sifted
125ml (4fl oz) whipping cream,
  whipped to soft peaks
120g (4oz) fresh raspberries

You will need a loose-bottomed 20cm (8in) round cake tin, brushed with melted butter and dusted with caster sugar

Athol Brose

**A Scottish dish. Brose is a word which
indicates oatmeal mixed with various other
things – water, milk, cream, whisky – to make
something in between a drink, a dessert and
a pick-me-up, depending on the nature and
proportions of the ingredients. This is a
rich one, suitable for dessert.**

Put the oatmeal in a bowl and add the water. Mix well
and leave to stand for about 30 minutes. Then strain
through a sieve, pressing to extract the creamy liquid
from the mixture. Reserve this and discard the oatmeal.
Mix the whisky, honey and lemon juice into the liquid.

Whisk the cream until stiff and stir most of it into the
whisky/honey mixture. Divide between four glasses.

Toast the remaining 2 tablespoons of oatmeal in a low
oven until lightly browned and nutty. Allow to cool, then
stir most of it into the remaining cream and use this to top
the mixture in the glasses. Scatter a few grains of toasted
oatmeal over the top to decorate.

SERVES 4

60g (2oz) medium oatmeal,
  plus about 2 tablespoons
  to finish the dish
125ml (4fl oz) water
2–4 tablespoons whisky
2 tablespoons heather honey
1 tablespoon lemon juice
125ml (4fl oz) whipping cream

Hatted Kit

An old-fashioned Scottish dish of curds, eclipsed by the popularity of yoghurt. The original ingredients were buttermilk from the churn and a cow, to be milked directly into the buttermilk – both now presenting difficulties unless you actually happen to own a cow. An approximation is possible with cultured buttermilk, but it needs a little help.

SERVES 6 AS A DESSERT

500ml (18fl oz) buttermilk
juice of ½ lemon
500ml (18fl oz) whole milk

Put the buttermilk and lemon juice in a pan and heat together to blood heat. Pour into a large jug or bowl. Put the milk in the pan (no need to rinse in between) and heat this to blood heat as well. Pour into the warm buttermilk in a thin stream, whisking the mixture as you do so. Cover and leave overnight at cool room temperature.

Next morning, the mixture should have separated into a thick curd (the 'hat') on top of thin whey. Line a clean sieve with a piece of scalded butter muslin and place over a bowl. Pour the mixture in and leave to drain for 4–5 hours. Discard the whey and store the curds in a covered bowl in the fridge.

They can be eaten as a savoury spread on brown bread with a little salt, or as a dessert with caster sugar. The sweetened version was traditionally sprinkled with a little grated nutmeg or powdered cinnamon, either of which are good; or serve with soft fruit such as raspberries.

Junket

Simple and good, this recipe is much nicer in individual dishes than as one large bowlful. This version is sometimes called Devon junket.

Heat the milk to blood heat. Dissolve the sugar in it, and stir in the brandy. Consult the instructions for the rennet and stir in the correct amount. Quickly divide the mixture between the glasses or dishes, and leave to set in a cool place.

Just before serving, add a teaspoon of sugar and a dust of cinnamon to the top of each portion. Add a little clotted cream for a really rich version.

SERVES 6

500ml (18fl oz) Channel
Island milk
1 heaped dessertspoon
caster sugar
2 tablespoons brandy
rennet
caster sugar, ground cinnamon
and clotted cream (optional)
to serve

You will need 6 ramekin dishes or tumblers

Cambridge Cheese

Making and selling cheese was one way a farmer's wife generated income for herself. Few traditional British recipes for cheese are suitable for urban settings in which the ingredients have to be purchased, but this, used in the Fens to the east of Cambridge until the mid-20th century, can be made quickly, in small quantities, and is delicious. Make it in summer, when the weather is settled and warm.

Crème fraîche gives a slight sourness when relying on pasteurised milk, and imitates a natural souring which develops in unpasteurised milk, or which is induced by cheese-makers with 'starters' of specially cultured bacteria.

You will need a deep metal or plastic tray, a solid wood or plastic board to fit inside it, a sushi mat and some moulds. Traditionally oblong wooden moulds were used. Now that the country craftsmen who used to make such objects have all disappeared, you have to improvise. 850ml (1½ pint) foil pudding moulds work quite well, even if the end result is not a traditional shape. Punch 8–10 evenly spaced holes, 5mm (¼in) in diameter, round the sides of each mould.

The process takes around 3 days.

1.5 litres (2½ pints) whole milk
100ml (3½fl oz) whipping cream
100ml (3½fl oz) full-fat crème fraîche
1 teaspoon rennet

Start the cheese first thing in the morning. Wash the tray, board, sushi mat and moulds thoroughly with boiling water. Don't add detergent, as it can taint the cheese. Put the board on the tray, cover with the mat, and have the moulds ready.

Mix the milk, cream and crème fraîche in a bowl then pour into a large pan and heat to blood temperature, (think baby milk temperature). Pour the mixture back into the bowl, add the rennet and stir a few times. Then leave strictly alone for 30 minutes. Press the top gently with a clean finger: it should have set to a firm junket. Carefully spoon this curd into the moulds, dividing it equally between them. Lots of whey will flow out of the moulds in the first few hours; carefully empty this off. Cover the moulds with a clean cloth and leave for 2–3 days, occasionally checking the amount of whey and emptying the tray if necessary. If you have a clean tray, carefully move the board carrying the moulds into it and wash the first one – cleanliness is essential with soft cheeses.

At the end of 3 days, unmould the little cheeses; they should have a slightly acid taste and a delicious rich texture. Since they are unsalted, they can be served either with fruit and sugar as a dessert, or with salad and biscuits as a light lunch or a starter. Keep refridgerated and eat within 2–3 days.

Teatime Treats

Bread, Tea Bread and Scones

Rye Bread

Flour is sold by a few National Trust tenants, especially in the South West, such as wholewheat flour suitable for bread that is milled at Dunster Watermill, Somerset. Rye and wheat were grown as a mixed crop known as maslin in the Middle Ages. In this recipe they make close-textured bread, good with butter and cheese.

Add the yeast to the warm water and leave it to work. Warm the milk. Mix the flours and salt in a bowl and add the honey. When the yeast is frothy mix all the ingredients together to make a dough and knead. Don't worry if it's slightly sticky. The ingredients can be mixed in a food processor, in which case they only need a minute to mix. Cover and leave to rise overnight – the dough will be fine left in a kitchen if it is cool, otherwise put it on the top shelf of the fridge.

Next morning, knock back the dough, flour a work surface and knead again. Shape into a loaf and put in the tin. Leave to prove for about an hour in a warm place.

Bake at 200°C, 400°F, Gas mark 6 for 15 minutes, then lower the heat to 190°C, 375°F, Gas mark 5 and bake for another 15 minutes. Turn the loaf out of the tin and return it to the oven, switched off, for a further 10 minutes, then allow to cool.

MAKES 1 LOAF

1 dessertspoon dried yeast
60ml (2fl oz) warm water
250ml (9fl oz) milk
250g (9oz) rye flour
250g (9oz) wholemeal flour,
    plus a little for dusting
1 teaspoon salt
30g (1oz) honey
lard, butter or oil for greasing

You will need a 900g (2lb)
loaf tin, lightly greased

Barley Bread

A close-textured bread devised by Bobby Freeman, using the traditional Welsh staple of barley flour. Barley lacks gluten, so this bread will not rise like a conventional loaf.

Cream the yeast with the molasses, sugar or honey and a little of the warm water. When it forms a frothy head, pour it into a bowl with the barley flour, oil and salt. Mix, adding more water as required to form a coherent but not sticky dough. Knead it for a few minutes, then leave in a warm place to rise for about 1½ hours.

Knock back, knead again, and place in the loaf tin. Prove for an hour. Make a deep cut along the top of the loaf and open out a little with your hand. Bake for an hour at 220°C, 425°F, Gas mark 7. Cool on a wire rack.

MAKES 1 LOAF

1 scant tablespoon dried yeast
2 teaspoons molasses, sugar or honey
300ml (½ pint) warm water
500g (1lb 2oz) barley flour
1 scant tablespoon vegetable oil
1 dessertspoon salt

You will need a 900g (2lb) loaf tin, lightly greased

Wheaten Bread

A recipe perhaps better known in Britain as 'soda bread' and closely associated with Irish food. Quick and easy to make, this is best made with wholemeal flour – look for a low-protein, coarse-ground, wholemeal flour, and avoid soda bread 'mixes'. This is easy to buy in Ireland, but more difficult in mainland Britain. Nora Brown, in a leaflet about Ulster breads, suggests adding 30g (1oz) oatmeal and 30g (1oz) brown sugar, and gives an alternative method of baking, which is to put the dough in a tin greased heavily with butter to give a nice crust.

If you can't get buttermilk an approximation – no more – can be made by thinning a little Greek yoghurt with milk and adding a spoonful of sour cream to give a mixture with a texture resembling single cream.

Mix the flour, salt and bicarbonate of soda in a bowl. Add the cream of tartar to the buttermilk and stir this mixture into the dry ingredients. Mix quickly but thoroughly to make a slightly wet dough. Turn onto a well-floured surface and cut in half. Shape each piece into a round, cut a cross halfway through the top of each and place on a floured baking tray. Bake immediately at 200°C, 400°F, Gas mark 6 for 30–40 minutes.

Soda bread goes stale quickly, so try to use it within 24 hours.

MAKES 2 SMALL LOAVES

500g (1lb 2oz) wholemeal flour, plus a little extra for dusting
1 teaspoon salt
1 teaspoon bicarbonate of soda
1½ teaspoons cream of tartar
400ml (14fl oz) buttermilk

Kentish Huffkins

Small breads are made all over Britain. The recipes vary in small details and the names are often intriguing. This is the Kent version of fine white rolls.

Add the sugar and yeast to the warm milk and set aside for a few minutes until it forms a frothy head. Mix the salt into the flour and rub in the lard. Stir in the yeast mixture and mix to form a dough, adding a little water if necessary. Knead for 10 minutes, then put the dough in an oiled bowl and cover with a damp cloth. Allow to rise in a warm place until doubled in size, for about 1 hour.

Knock back and divide into 12 pieces. Roll each one out into an oval about 12cm (5in) long. Place on greased baking trays and make a hole in the centre of each oval. Flour well and prove until well risen. Bake in a hot oven, 220°C, 425°F, Gas mark 7 for 15–20 minutes. Wrap in a warm cloth to preserve the soft crust as they cool.

MAKES 12

1 teaspoon granulated sugar
1 dessertspoon dried yeast
250ml (9fl oz) hand-hot milk
½ teaspoon salt
500g (about 1lb) strong
    plain flour
30g (1oz) lard

Cornish Splits

A Cornish version of little breads as recorded by Florence White in the 1930s. These rolls are delicious with clotted cream and jam.

Cream the yeast with the sugar in the warm milk. Gently melt the butter and lard and add to the flour, together with the yeast mixture. Sprinkle in the salt. Add enough of the tepid water to make a dough. Knead for about 10 minutes, cover and put in a warm place to rise. When doubled in size, knock back and knead again. Divide into 50g (1½oz) pieces and shape into rolls. Place on a greased baking tray and allow to prove. Bake at 220°C, 425°F, Gas mark 7 for 20 minutes. On removing the rolls from the oven, rub over with a butter paper and then wrap in a cloth to cool.

1 tablespoon dried yeast
1 teaspoon granulated sugar
60ml (2fl oz) hand-hot milk
120g (4oz) butter, plus a little
 extra for greasing
30g (1oz) lard
750g (1lb 10oz) strong plain flour
1 teaspoon salt
400ml (14fl oz) tepid water

Sally Lunn

There is no consensus on how this rich bread, associated with the town of Bath, got its curious name. What matters is that it tastes good and shouldn't be ignored just because commercial bakers have developed an obsession with foccacia.

Mix the yeast, water and sugar together and set aside until it froths. Beat in the cream, egg, yolk and lemon. Put the flour in a mixing bowl and add the salt. Stir in the yeast mixture and mix everything well together. The mixture is too sticky to knead, but you should be able to form it into a flat round on a well-floured surface. Put the round of dough into the buttered tin. Leave in a warm place to rise for 1–1½ hours.

Bake at 200°C, 400°F, Gas mark 6 for 15 minutes; if the bun seems a bit pale, turn the oven down to 170°C, 325°F, Gas mark 3 and give it an extra 5 minutes.

The proper way to eat Sally Lunns is to tear them in half, butter very liberally, put the halves back together and return the bread to the oven for a few minutes to melt the butter. Clotted cream can be used instead of butter.

1 teaspoon dried yeast
75ml (2½fl oz) warm water
pinch of sugar
125ml (4fl oz) single cream
1 whole egg and 1 egg yolk
grated zest of ¼ lemon
250g (9oz) strong plain flour
½ teaspoon salt
butter for greasing

You will need a deep cake tin, 15cm (6in) in diameter, lightly greased

Teacakes

My grandmother's recipe for a type of little bread well known in Yorkshire.

Mix the yeast with 100ml (3½fl oz) tepid water and set aside until frothy. Put the flour, sugar and salt in a bowl and rub in the lard. Add the dried fruit. Pour in the yeast mixture and stir; add another 100ml (3½fl oz) water and keep mixing to form a dough, adding more water if necessary. Knead well, then cover and set aside to rise.

When doubled in size, knock back and divide into 8 pieces. Flatten each one into a disc 10–12cm (4–5in) in diameter. Place on greased baking trays and allow to prove. When nicely risen, bake at 220°C, 425°F, Gas mark 7 for 10–15 minutes.

Eat warm with butter, or allow to cool, split and toast.

MAKES 8

1 teaspoon dried yeast
about 250ml (9fl oz) tepid water
500g (about 1lb) plain flour
30g (1oz) sugar
pinch of salt
30g (1oz) lard
30g (1oz) currants
30g (1oz) raisins

Wigs

A 'wig' was the name given to a small bread roll from the late Middle Ages well into the 19th century. They were usually a little richer than plain bread, and both Kendal and Hawkshead were noted for them, although they now seem to be forgotten. A shame, because they are good. This recipe from the Lake District was recorded by Florence White.

Add a pinch of sugar to the warm water and set the yeast to work until frothy. Put the flour and salt in a bowl and rub in the lard. Stir in the sugar and caraway seeds. Add the yeast mixture, the milk, and a little more water if necessary to make a dough. Knead well, then leave to rise in a warm place.

When doubled in size, knock back and divide into 16 pieces. Roll each into a small, flat round and place on a greased baking tray. Allow to prove, then bake at 180°C, 350°F, Gas mark 4 for 15–20 minutes.

MAKES 16

100ml (3½fl oz) warm water
2 teaspoons dried yeast
500g (about 1lb) strong
   plain flour
½ teaspoon salt
50g (1¾oz) lard
50g (1¾oz) soft light brown sugar
1 tablespoon caraway seeds
150ml (5fl oz) milk

Staffordshire or Derbyshire Oatcakes

A traditional food of the Peak District and the Potteries: pancake-like, thin and floppy. They were, and still are in the Potteries towns, made by specialists, but are also quite simple to make at home. The important point is to get the batter the right consistency.

MAKES 7–8

1 teaspoon dried yeast
400ml (14fl oz) hand-hot water
100g (3½oz) fine oatmeal
40g (1½oz) plain flour
pinch of salt
lard, vegetable oil or dripping
    for frying

Stir the yeast into the water, then add all the other ingredients and whisk to make a smooth batter as thick as double cream. Leave in a warm place for an hour.

Heat a heavy frying pan, or a hotplate or girdle if you have one (see page 11), on top of the stove. Grease it very lightly. Pour on enough batter to form a circle 16–17cm (6½in) in diameter and let it cook gently. A few holes will appear in the top, which takes on a drier, set appearance. When the edges begin to lift a little, slide a spatula underneath the cake and flip it over. Allow to cook for a few minutes longer and then remove to a wire rack. Make all the pancakes this way. They can be stored in the fridge for 48 hours.

To serve, reheat either by frying in bacon fat and dishing up with a fried breakfast, or toasting both sides lightly under the grill and spreading with a little butter and some heather honey.

Pikelets

These are similar in concept to Staffordshire and Derbyshire oatcakes (see previous page) and relatives of Welsh crempog (see page 218). This version is from the Peak District (see following page for more on farmhouse produce from this area). Much better than anything you can buy in the shops, eat them buttered for breakfast or tea.

Sieve the flour into a large bowl, make a well in the centre and sprinkle the salt round the edge. Warm the milk to hand-hot in a pan and add the yeast. When it is frothy, pour into the flour and stir in, adding the eggs. Beat well to make a runny batter. Cover and leave in a warm place for 1–2 hours.

Heat a hotplate, girdle or heavy frying pan, grease it with a little butter, drop the batter in spoonfuls and cook until numerous holes appear in the top. Flip over with a spatula and cook briefly on the other side, until lightly browned. Toast under the grill before serving.

MAKES 24

200g (7oz) plain flour
1 scant teaspoon salt
300ml (½ pint) milk
½ teaspoon dried yeast
2 eggs
butter for greasing

Farmhouse Cookery in the Peak District

The Peak District packs a lot of scenery into a small area, with two completely contrasting landscapes – the High or Dark Peak in the north and the White Peak to the south-east. The Dark Peak includes two high, brooding gritstone hills, Bleaklow and Kinder Scout, vast flat expanses of spongy peat bog, heather moorland and coarse grass with occasional weather-worn rock formations. The deep 'cloughs' or valleys contain square fields divided by charcoal-grey dry-stone walls and the occasional isolated farm. The White Peak has a completely different character – the underlying limestone gives vivid green pastures divided by pale stone walls. The streams here often vanish into underground caves, and some of the narrow little valleys are actually collapsed caverns. This area was mined for lead in the past, and in some places 'rakes' – ridges and spoil heaps created by mining – are evident. The spoil contains enough lead to be poisonous to grazing animals, and is sometimes tree-planted to prevent browsing. To the south-west lies an area of more mixed countryside. Hedged meadows and pastures fill the valleys running down to the flat land of Cheshire, Shropshire and Staffordshire. Higher up, moorland with gritstone walls and outcrops such as the long spiky ridge of The Roaches occupies the north-east of Staffordshire. With the Potteries towns to the west, Manchester to the north-west, and Sheffield, Nottingham and Derby to the east, the Peak District is a popular destination for a day out.

This area marks the beginning of the Pennine hills, which stretch north to the Scottish border, and in common with much hill land, grazing of cattle and

Old Park Hill and the Hamps Valley in the South Peak Estate area of the Peak District National Park.

sheep is important. In the harsh environment of the Dark Peak, the higher ground is given over to managed heather moorland for grouse shooting. The south-western peak, with better pastures, produces sheep and cattle, and has some dairy farms. Dairying is much more important in the White Peak. Stilton cheese originated in Leicestershire in the 18th century and has been made at Hartington in Dovedale for at least a century. Another important Midlands tradition is the raised pork pie.

Sadly, the herb-rich fields with their beautiful spring flowers, characteristic of the limestone peak, have mostly vanished because of late 20th-century ideas about grassland management, but an interest in plants and their properties seems to be a feature of the area. The most vivid expression of this is the well-dressings, pictures and patterns made from leaves and petals impressed into clay, which several villages create every spring.

Like all farming communities, the Peak District favours home-baking. The climate in this area is too cool and wet to grow good wheat so oats are an important ingredient. Staffordshire and Derbyshire share a tradition of making large, yeast-leavened oatcakes, generally bought from shops that specialise in them. Oatmeal also goes into thor or thar cake, a relative of Yorkshire parkin (see page 254). Pikelets, based on wheat flour, and made thick or thin, are also traditional. Bakewell pudding, bought in the town or made at home, was for special occasions and for 'wakes', the local name for a fair.

Crempog

These little breads were made on the *planc*, an iron baking sheet that every Welsh household possessed. They were also known as *leicecs* or lightcakes, and were a tea-time tradition for guests in parts of north and central Wales. Simple and very delicious, they'd be good for breakfast or brunch.

Mix the flour, sugar and salt in a small bowl. Add the sour cream or yoghurt and mix. Break in the egg and stir vigorously to make a smooth batter. Blend in the milk. You should have a batter which drops nicely off the spoon. This much can be done in advance.

Just before cooking, set a heavy iron frying pan or *planc* to heat, or use a hotplate if your cooker has one. It needs to be quite hot and well greased.

Mix the cream of tartar and bicarbonate of soda in a small bowl and add a tablespoon of water. Immediately pour the mixture into the batter and stir well.

Drop the batter in tablespoons on the hot pan or *planc*. When the underside is golden and the top full of little holes, flip over with a spatula and cook for a moment on the other side. Serve immediately with butter.

MAKES 18

100g (3½oz) plain flour
40g (1½oz) caster sugar
pinch of salt
60g (2oz) sour cream or
    plain yoghurt
1 egg
100ml (3½fl oz) milk, or
    buttermilk if available
lard or fat for greasing
1 teaspoon cream of tartar
1 teaspoon bicarbonate of soda
salty butter to serve

Saffron Cake

Not a cake in the modern sense, but a traditionally Cornish fruit bread lightly spiced with saffron.

Put the saffron in the boiling water and leave to infuse overnight. Mix 100g (3½oz) of the flour, a pinch of sugar, the yeast and the tepid water, and leave it for about 30 minutes until frothy.

Rub the fat into the remaining flour. Add the salt, sugar and egg, the yeast mixture and the saffron water. Mix to a coherent dough, adding a little more tepid water if necessary. Knead well, cover the bowl with clingfilm and leave to rise in a warm place for about an hour.

Knock back and knead in the fruit and peel. Place in the greased loaf tin and prove for about an hour.

Bake at 220°C, 425°F, Gas mark 7 for 40 minutes, or until the loaf sounds hollow when tapped on the base. Cool on a wire rack. Eat thinly sliced, spread with butter.

a generous pinch of
 saffron threads
3 tablespoons boiling water
500g (1lb 2oz) strong plain
 white flour
100g (3½oz) sugar
1 tablespoon dried yeast
100ml (3½fl oz) tepid water
100g (3½oz) lard or butter
1 teaspoon salt
1 egg, beaten
250g (9oz) currants
30g (1oz) candied peel, chopped

You will need a 1.2 litre (2 pint) loaf tin, greased

Ellerbeck Spice Bread

The range of breads once made in Britain varied much more than the bakery products that line today's supermarket shelves could ever show. Several different grains – oats, barley, rye, wheat, and mixtures of these – were used for bread (recipes using these have been included in this book). In parts of Britain, these recipes were used well into the 20th century, and some still are used.

Wheat makes the lightest bread, although the quality of English-grown wheat over the centuries has often been debated by historians (work done on DNA extracted from late medieval wheat grains preserved in ancient thatch at the National Trust's Holnicote Estate suggests it could be very good for bread-making). It was always the choice for the many types of small bread rolls associated with different areas of the country, and for festive breads made with butter, eggs, sugar and dried fruit. Historically, these were the ancestors of fruit cakes. Spice bread, as it was made in Yorkshire until the mid-20th century, is a survival of these – the ingredients showing a relationship to fruit cakes, but maintaining the old habit of raising with yeast rather than baking powder. It was made specially for Christmas.

MAKES 1 LOAF

1 dessertspoon dried yeast
200ml (7fl oz) hand-hot milk
150g (5oz) demerara sugar
325g (11oz) strong plain flour
½ teaspoon salt
1 teaspoon mixed sweet spice
120g (4oz) butter
120g (4oz) currants
60g (2oz) sultanas
30g (1oz) mixed candied peel
1 egg

You will need a 900g (2lb) loaf tin, greased and lined

This recipe was collected in the 1930s by Mrs Arthur Webb. Ellerbeck lies on the eastern edge of the Cleveland Hills in North Yorkshire.

Whisk the yeast into 100ml (3½fl oz) milk with a pinch of sugar, and set aside until frothy. Mix the flour, salt, sugar and spice. Rub in the butter – not as thoroughly as for pastry, just until it is well distributed. Make a well in the middle and pour in the yeast mixture. Stir in a little of the flour from around the edge and leave it to work for a further 20 minutes. Then mix to a dough, adding the milk as necessary. Knead well, place in an oiled bowl, cover with a damp cloth and leave in a warm place for an hour or so. The mixture is unlikely to rise much.

Knock back and knead in the fruit, peel and egg. Shape into a loaf and place in the prepared loaf tin. Allow to prove for an hour; again, it won't rise very much. Bake at 180°C, 350°F, Gas mark 4 for 1 hour and 20 minutes; test with a skewer, and bake a little longer if necessary. Cool on a wire rack, slice and spread with butter.

Fruit Loaf

Peggy Ellwood donated this recipe for a plain but very good fruit loaf of a type well known in the Lake District, in which the dried fruit is soaked in tea before the loaf is mixed.

The night before you want to make the loaf, pour the tea over the dried fruit and leave to soak.

Next day, add all the other ingredients and mix well. Pour into the loaf tin and bake on the middle shelf of the oven at 170°C, 325°F, Gas mark 3 for 1½–2 hours. Leave to cool in the tin. Slice and serve well buttered.

MAKES 1 LOAF

300ml (½ pint) strong tea
450g (1lb) mixed dried fruit, such as sultanas, raisins and currants
175g (6oz) soft light brown sugar
350g (12oz) self-raising flour
2 large eggs, beaten
3 tablespoons milk
2–3 drops vanilla essence and a little mixed spice (optional)

You will need a 900g (2lb) loaf tin, well greased and lined

Bara Brith

Bara Brith means 'speckled bread' in Welsh and it is another variation of the fruit bread theme so common in Britain. It should be noted that it works better with really good raisins.

Warm the milk, add a pinch of sugar and the yeast. Mix the flour, brown sugar, salt and spice, and rub in the fat roughly. Stir in the dried fruit and peel. Add the yeast mixture and the egg and mix to a dough, adding a little more water or milk if necessary. Knead well, then allow to rise until doubled in size, this may take 2 hours.

Knock back, divide into 2 pieces and shape each into a loaf. Place in the loaf tins and prove until well risen.

Bake at 200°C, 400°F, Gas mark 6 for 15 minutes, then lower the heat to 180°C, 350°F, Gas mark 4 and cook for a further 40–45 minutes, or until the loaves sound hollow when tapped underneath. Best kept for a couple of days before cutting. Serve buttered.

MAKES 2 LOAVES

100ml (3½fl oz) milk
pinch of granulated sugar
1 scant tablespoon yeast
500g (1lb 2oz) strong plain flour
120g (4oz) soft brown sugar
½ teaspoon salt
½ teaspoon mixed spice
120g (4oz) lard or butter,
   or a mixture of both
175g (6oz) good-quality raisins
175g (6oz) currants
60g (2oz) mixed candied
   peel, chopped
1 egg

You will need two 1.2 litre (2 pint) loaf tins, greased

Barm Brack

This recipe comes with apologies to the contemporary Ulster baking tradition, which now relies on cream of tartar and bicarbonate of soda to raise breads and cakes of all kinds. It dates to 1825, before chemical raising agents were available. No apologies for the results, which are superb. For more information on traditional farmhouse produce from Northern Ireland, see the following page.

Set the yeast to work with the warm water and a pinch of sugar. Mix the flour, sugar, salt and seeds. Warm the milk to hand-hot and melt the butter in it. Beat in the egg. Mix this into the flour to make a dough, adding a little more milk or water if necessary. Knead well, place in a bowl and allow to rise in a warm place for 3 hours.

Knock back, put into a greased cake tin and prove for about 40 minutes.

Bake at 200°C, 400°F, Gas mark 6 for 20 minutes, then lower the heat to 180°C, 350°F, Gas mark 4 and bake for a further 15–20 minutes. If the base of the cake sounds hollow when tapped, it is done. Turn out and cool on a wire rack.

Excellent with butter and cheese.

1 dessertspoon dried yeast
60ml (2fl oz) warm water
60g (2oz) caster sugar
500g (1lb 2oz) plain flour
1 scant teaspoon salt
15g (½oz) caraway seeds
250ml (8½fl oz) hand-hot milk
40g (1½oz) butter, plus extra
    for greasing
1 egg

**You will need a 20cm (8in)
diameter cake tin**

Farmhouse Cookery in Northern Ireland

There are two words everyone associates with the Irish countryside: green and damp. The green comes in many shades – yellowish, for a new-mown hay meadow, emerald for the pastures, deep viridian for late summer trees and hedges. There are other colours too – the black and white of basalt and chalk at the Giant's Causeway, the wine of heather in bloom, the brilliant acid-yellow of gorse in flower, smoky blues of mountains in the distance and of loughs reflecting the sky, which may be anything from the palest limpid blue to lowering steel-grey As for the damp, that's what keeps the landscape green. The province of Northern Ireland is the most north-eastern part of Ireland, a rough circle from Belfast round through the clear waters and green islets of Strangford Lough, past the mountains of Mourne to Newry. From here the border with southern Ireland winds inland to the west to take in Upper and Lower Lough Erne, and then returns northwards to Londonderry. The scenery of the northern coast is spectacularly beautiful, with the Glens of Antrim and on the coast the Giant's Causeway offering a particularly pleasing combination of land and water, with flat green fields divided by walls. Inland are the heather and tawny grass of the Sperrin Mountains and the expanse of Lough Neagh. To the south of this Counties Tyrone and Armagh provide lush arable farmland. The prevailing westerly winds bring rain only, no pollution, and the air and waterways are very clean.

Northern Irish food, while obviously related to that of mainland Britain, has its own characteristics. The greenness of the countryside is reflected in the grass-fed beef and lamb from the Antrim Hills and the Sperrin Mountains. The beef is reared with particular care, and farmers in Northern Ireland introduced a traceability scheme to assure quality and safety well before those on the UK mainland. Pork is eaten, fresh or as ham or bacon, in a piece, or in rashers, as part of the 'Ulster fry', the Northern Irish version of the cooked breakfast. There is also a strong tradition of hunting and eating game – pheasants, pigeons, venison and, for those lucky enough to live in the south-westernmost corner, snipe. Fish, both from the sea and from inland waters, is an essential part of the diet.

Armagh is Northern Ireland's orchard county, producing apples and strawberries. Making jams and chutneys is part of the domestic tradition. A limited selection of good vegetables, especially root crops, is grown and used in the kitchen. Potatoes are by far the most important, and the Irish kitchen as a whole includes a remarkable variety of potato dishes. They do well in the mild damp climate as, sadly, does potato blight, which precipitated the disastrous famine of the 1840s.

The other great products of the land are butter and the buttermilk left over from churning (see previous page for a traditional Irish recipe using these typical ingredients). Butter is used for frying, baking, on bread and mixed into potatoes. Buttermilk gives a unique touch to several Irish breads and potato dishes, and really is essential for texture and flavour. With such an emphasis on butter, cheese has never been very important, although some Irish farmers, like their counterparts in Britain, have worked creatively with continental traditions of cheese-making.

The home-baking tradition, both for bread and fancier items, is alive and well. Bread is routinely made at home. Yeast is now not used in Northern Irish baking, but soda bread and wheaten (wholemeal) bread raised with bicarbonate of soda and buttermilk or cream of tartar are well known outside the territory.

A pig on Bally Quintin Farm, Northern Ireland.

Devon Scones

Devon traditions included little bread rolls known as chudleighs, similar to Cornish splits (see page 208), but scones seem to have taken their place.

Sieve the dry ingredients together. Rub in the butter. Stir in the milk to make a soft, slightly sticky dough. Flour your hands and a work surface and press the dough together. Roll out to about 2cm (¾in) thick and use a 5cm (2in) round cutter to cut scones. Place on a lightly floured baking tray and bake at 220°C, 425°F, Gas mark 7 for 10 minutes.

MAKES 16 SMALL FLUFFY SCONES

250g (9oz) plain flour,
    plus extra for dusting
1 teaspoon bicarbonate
    of soda
2 teaspoons cream of tartar
½ teaspoon salt
2 teaspoons caster sugar
30g (1oz) butter
200ml (7fl oz) milk

Brown Scones

Excellent served with sour cream and smoked fish – try these scones with Craster kippers from the Northumberland coast.

Sieve the dry ingredients together. Rub in the lard or butter. Beat the egg and stir in, and add enough milk to make a coherent dough. Divide the dough into two equal pieces and form each into a neat square, rolling out to about 1cm (½in) thick. Trim the edges so they are reasonably neat, then place each piece on a greased baking tray and cut into nine square scones. Bake at 220°C, 425°F, Gas mark 7 for 10 minutes. Eat warm.

MAKES 18 SMALL SCONES

200g (7oz) wholemeal flour
200g (7oz) plain flour
1 teaspoon bicarbonate
   of soda
1 teaspoon cream of tartar
generous pinch of salt
100g (3½oz) lard or butter
1 egg
4–6 tablespoons milk

Cream Scones

A 'north country' recipe, originally given by Florence White.

Rub the butter into the flour. Stir in the salt and the raising agents. Beat the eggs and cream together and stir in. Add enough milk to make a soft but not sticky dough and knead lightly.

Roll out to approximately 2cm (¾in) thick and cut in rounds. Bake at 220°C, 425°F, Gas mark 7 for about 15 minutes.

60g (2oz) butter
500g (about 1lb) self-raising flour
1 teaspoon salt
1 teaspoon cream of tartar
½ teaspoon bicarbonate of soda
2 eggs
150ml (¼ pint) double cream
about 200ml (7fl oz) milk, to mix

Barley Bannocks

Traditional Scottish baking is fascinating both for the different flours which were used, and for the technique of girdle baking for all sorts of small breads, pancakes and scones. The original of this recipe was given by F. Marian MacNeill. I suggest the mixture should be rolled very thin, to make a delicious pancake-like bread.

Put the milk, butter and salt in a pan and heat. As soon as it comes to the boil, remove it from the heat and stir in the barley flour to make a paste (it may take a little more flour than the quantity stated, but shouldn't be dry). Turn it on to a work surface, press together and allow to cool a little.

Gently heat a girdle or a heavy cast-iron frying pan on top of the stove, to be ready when you have rolled the first bannock. Divide the mixture into six, and roll the first portion out into a thin circle. It will be quite difficult to handle, especially if the mixture is still quite warm. Dust the work surface and rolling pin liberally with flour, and don't worry too much about it tearing. Make it about 5mm (¼in) thick, pick it up on the rolling pin and transfer to the heated girdle or pan. Turn the heat up a little and let it cook fairly quickly. Keep lifting the edge with a spatula to check on progress: when the underneath is nicely cooked with lots of brown spots, carefully turn it over and cook the other side.

While it bakes, roll out the next bannock, ready to go on the girdle when the first one is done.

Eat hot with butter and cheese, or soup. Any left can be dried (leave them on the girdle as it cools) to give a slightly biscuity, crisp result, still good the next day.

MAKES 6

400ml (14fl oz) whole milk
40g (1½oz) butter
pinch of salt
about 200g (7oz) barley flour,
    plus extra for rolling out

You will need a girdle (iron baking sheet) or a heavy cast-iron frying pan

Oat Bannocks

A more traditional Scottish style of bannock, made thicker. This is based on a mixture of oat and wheat flour.

Sieve the flour, oatmeal, baking powder and salt together. Rub in the butter, then stir in the sugar and milk to make a malleable but not too sticky dough. Knead lightly, then shape into a bannock about 2cm (¾in) thick.

Heat the girdle and put the bannock on it immediately, cutting it across into 4 wedges. Allow to cook gently for about 10 minutes, until lightly browned, then turn each quarter and allow about another 10 minutes or until done.

Like barley bannock, this is good with butter, cheese, or soup.

SERVES 4

150g (5oz) plain flour,
   plus extra for rolling out
100g (4oz) fine oatmeal
1 teaspoon baking powder
about ½ teaspoon salt
butter
15g (½oz) sugar
about 150ml (¼ pint) milk

You will need a girdle (iron baking sheet) or a heavy cast-iron frying pan

Soda Farls

Another bread associated with Northern Ireland. Delicious for tea with butter and jam, or for breakfast with scrambled eggs, and maybe some smoked trout.

Sieve the flour, baking powder and salt into a bowl. Add the buttermilk and stir well to make a soft dough (you may need to add a little more liquid). Turn the dough onto a well-floured surface and work briefly to make sure everything is well mixed. The dough should be quite sticky. Pat out into a circle 1cm (½in) thick.

Heat the hotplate or frying pan gently. Sprinkle lightly with flour. When the flour begins to brown lightly, place the circle of dough onto it. Pat down lightly and cut into quarters. Cook gently and try not to let it scorch. After about 10 minutes, turn each quarter over in the pan; the cooked side should have golden-brown patches on it. Cook for a further 5–7 minutes. Serve straight away for breakfast or tea, with butter and jam.

200g (7oz) plain, unbleached white flour, plus extra for dusting
1 teaspoon baking powder
½ teaspoon salt
150ml (¼ pint) buttermilk (see page 206 for more information)

You will need a hotplate or a large, heavy frying pan

Norfolk Rusks

These little bread rolls are unusual in English bread-making, but are a well-established recipe in Norfolk.

Rub the butter into the flour. Mix in the salt and baking powder. Add the egg and stir well, then add enough milk to make a fairly stiff paste. Divide into 18 pieces and roll each into a round 1cm (½in) thick. Place on a greased baking sheet and bake at 220°C, 425°F, Gas mark 7 for 5–7 minutes until well risen. Remove from the oven and allow to cool for a short time, then score round the middle with a knife and pull each one in half.

Return to a cool oven at 150°C, 300°F, Gas mark 2 until golden and dry all the way through (this takes about an hour). Cool and store in an airtight container. Eat with butter.

MAKES 18

100g (3½oz) butter
200g (7oz) plain flour
½ teaspoon salt
1 teaspoon baking powder
1 egg
2 tablespoons milk

Mrs Ingleby's Oatcakes

An early 20th-century recipe from Littondale in Yorkshire, given to my mother by a local farmer's wife. Eat with butter or cheese.

Put the dry ingredients in a bowl and rub in the lard or butter. Add the buttermilk or yoghurt and mix to a stiff dough. Press together and cut into three equal pieces. Roll each piece out to 5mm (¼in) thick. Slide onto a baking tray (no need to grease) and cut each into 12. Bake at 180°C, 350°F, Gas mark 4 for about 15 minutes.

Cool on a wire rack and store in an airtight container.

MAKES 36

300g (10oz) medium oatmeal
150g (5oz) plain flour
½ teaspoon salt
75g (2½oz) lard or butter
4–5 tablespoons buttermilk
  (yoghurt is a good substitute
  if this is not available)

Cakes and Biscuits

Shrewsbury Cakes

Recipes for these cakes, named for Shrewsbury in the heart of the Welsh Marches, have changed over the years from thick, delicately spiced shortcakes to biscuits with currants in them. This version is based on a recipe in a manuscript of 1847, with the addition of flavours that recall 18th-century recipes.

Mix the sugar and butter, stirring until well amalgamated and soft. Add the flour and spices, the egg yolk and the sherry and rosewater. Mix thoroughly. A little extra sherry or rosewater may be needed, but try not to let the dough become sticky. Allow the mixture to rest for half an hour.

Roll out on a floured surface to 5mm (¼in) thick and cut out rounds. Place on baking trays and bake at 170°C, 325°F, Gas mark 3 for about 15 minutes; try not to let them brown.

Transfer the biscuits to a wire rack; they will crisp up as they cool. Store in an airtight container.

MAKES 40

250g (9oz) caster sugar
250g (9oz) butter, softened
375g (13oz) plain flour
½ teaspoon ground cinnamon
½ teaspoon ground nutmeg
1 egg yolk
1 tablespoon sherry
1 tablespoon rosewater
    (or use extra sherry)
¼ teaspoon salt
caraway seeds (optional)

Mrs Watson's Iced Ginger Shortcake

Mrs Watson's family farm is in Northumberland, where the hills start to rise towards the Cheviots. These shortcake fingers are delicious.

Cream the butter with the caster sugar. Mix the flour with the ginger and work into the creamed mixture. Press into the tin and bake at 150–170°C, 300–325°F, Gas mark 2–3 for 40 minutes, until golden brown.

While the shortcake is still warm, make the icing. Melt the butter and syrup together. Add the ginger and icing sugar and stir thoroughly to give a smooth mixture with no white patches of icing sugar. Pour over the shortcake. Cut into fingers while still warm, then leave to cool in the tin.

MAKES 16 FINGERS

200g (7oz) butter
100g (3½oz) caster sugar
250g (9oz) flour (Mrs Watson
   recommends half plain, half
   self-raising)
1½ teaspoons ground ginger

FOR THE ICING
70g (2½oz) butter
1 tablespoon golden syrup
1 teaspoon ground ginger
60g (2oz) icing sugar

**You will need a shallow
22cm (8½in) square tin**

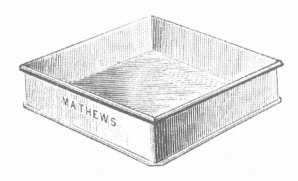

Strawberry Shortcake

Hampshire strawberries were famous, partly because they were the first to reach the London market in the days before imported ones became commonplace. The freshest, ripest strawberries are needed for this cake.

Mix the flour, sugar and salt. Rub in the butter, and stir in the beaten egg to make a soft, slightly sticky dough. Flour a work surface well, divide the dough in half and pat each one into a circle on a greased baking tray. Chill for an hour.

Bake at 170°C, 325°F, Gas mark 3 for 30–35 minutes, until lightly browned; if the mixture spreads a lot, neaten it by trimming with a sharp knife while still hot. Cool on wire racks. About 2 hours before eating, place one cake on a plate and cover with strawberries – cut very large ones in half – and put the other cake on top. Reserve a few fine berries for decoration.

Just before serving, whip the cream and spread over the top of the cake. Decorate with the reserved strawberries and serve.

175g (6oz) plain flour, plus
  extra for dusting
175g (6oz) caster sugar
pinch of salt
175g (6oz) butter
1 egg, beaten
750g (1lb 10oz) strawberries
100ml (3½fl oz) whipping cream

My Lady's Shortcake

Under this name, Mrs Arthur Webb gave instructions for one of our numerous variations on the theme of currants and pastry. It seems to be a relative of a Cornish cake known as 'heavy cake' or 'hevvas' – a concoction of butter or cream, flour and currants, but is lighter and more delicate.

Use the flour, butter and a little cold water to make up some shortcrust pastry (see page 13). Allow it to rest for 30 minutes in the fridge, then roll it into a neat square about 30 x 30cm (12 x 12in). It should be quite thin. Scatter the peel, currants and sultanas over the top, then sprinkle the sugar over. Turn in 1cm (½in) of pastry along each edge to contain the filling, then roll the pastry up like a Swiss roll. Roll out again, gently so that the fruit doesn't break the surface too much, to give an oblong of roughly the same dimensions as the original. Score the surface to give a diamond pattern.

Bake at 220°C, 425°F, Gas mark 7 for 10 minutes, then turn the oven down to 180°C, 350°F, Gas mark 4 and bake for another 15 minutes. Around 5 minutes before the end of cooking, brush the top with beaten egg so that it has a nice glaze.

200g (7oz) plain flour
100g (3½oz) butter
60g (2oz) mixed peel
60g (2oz) currants
60g (2oz) sultanas
2 tablespoons caster sugar
egg to glaze

Pitcaithly Bannock

This is a type of Scottish shortbread which includes almonds and candied peel. Shortbread should be an expression of the best of country produce – butter – combined with fine white flour and sugar (see following page for more information on traditional Scottish produce). We may now have too much of these, but historically they were expensive and desirable luxuries. The quality of the butter is of great importance; the better it is, the better the shortbread will be. Look for really good butter made from cream from whole milk, not whey butter made as a by-product of cheese-making (and don't even think about margarine). You may be lucky and find farm-made butter; otherwise, that made with the milk of Ayrshire, Guernsey or Jersey cattle is a good choice.

180g (6oz) flour
30g (1oz) rice flour, but if you can't get this, use an extra 30g (1oz) ordinary flour
30g (1oz) ground almonds
30g (1oz) candied citron or orange peel
120g (4oz) butter
90g (3oz) caster sugar

Dry the flour in a low oven (don't let it brown). Cool and sieve. Mix in the rice flour and ground almonds. Chop the candied peel very finely and add this to the flour.

Blend the butter and sugar until well mixed (traditionally this was done by rubbing them together on a board, but this is a potentially messy process, better done in a bowl unless you are used to the method). Work in the dry ingredients. Don't knead the mixture, but press it together into a ball.

Put this on a sheet of baking parchment on a baking tray. Press out to a circle about 20cm (8in) in diameter. Pinch the edges to make a decorative border.

Bake at 170°C, 350°F, Gas mark 3 for about 30 minutes, or until golden. Allow to cool on the tray until firm, then transfer to a wire rack.

Farmhouse Cookery in Scotland

Scotland is a country whose geology shows through in varied and beautiful landscapes: the steep-sided, rounded hills of the Borders, an empty landscape of cloud shadows flitting across grassy slopes; to the west the hills become darker, the soil thinner, the contours blurred by softer, sea-influenced light and lusher vegetation. The lower land between Edinburgh and Glasgow is rarely out of sight of hills, and moving north these reassert themselves, dramatically, along the ancient faultline which marks the edge of the Highlands.

Beyond this the scenery is the cliché of every shortbread tin lid. Impressive mountains, tree-hung or scattered with scree, rise to precipices above deeply cut glens, the base of each lined with flat green meadows and threaded with silver rivers or occupied by long narrow lochs. Under this lies a complex geology of ancient, acid rocks, smoothed and worn by the glaciers of the last ice age, and snow patches sometimes still last all year round in the corries of north-facing slopes. With subtle variations this sets the pattern for north and west Scotland. On the west coast slender, rocky promontories cradle sea lochs which open towards the islands of the Hebrides; to the north, beyond the horizon, lie first the flat Orkney Islands and then Shetland Islands. To the east, around the coast the undulating peat-bogs of the Flow country fade into the productive landscape of the Black Isle and the east coast generally. All regions have interesting dishes and food traditions, but perhaps this level, fertile area between the Highlands and the sea, studded with great houses, has most potential for a rich and well-rounded tradition of cookery.

Scotland is cattle country at heart. Tumbled shielings, once the summer quarters of herders, lie beside remote lochs and rivers, and green drove roads lead south towards former cattle markets in England. The pastoral tradition also provides recipes for dairy products and soft cheeses. Dairying for milk, butter and hard cheese is still important in Ayrshire, which gave its name to a bronze and white breed of dairy cattle. Other Scottish cattle breeds – hairy Highland cattle, tubby Galloways and black Aberdeen Angus – are prized for their superb beef, good as roasts, stews, soups and pies.

In the 19th century, first sheep farming, and then sporting estates for deer stalking and grouse shooting displaced cattle in the Highlands. Their produce probably did not make much of an impact on the diet of ordinary people, but red deer are now farmed and fallow and roe relatively common and their meat easily available. Fish has always been present: salmon is perhaps most obvious to us now, especially since the development of fish farming, but herring and seafish, fresh or smoked, are also important.

Despite the northerly latitude, the lower land along the east coast is good growing country, helped by the long daylight hours of summer. The fertile soil produces barley, oats and potatoes. A baking tradition still recalls the use of oats and barley for bannocks (small loaves), as well as wheat for breads large and small. Baking on a girdle to make small fresh unleavened breads for teatime is a skill which has not entirely vanished. Barley is also grown for beer and whisky. Soft fruit grows well, rows of strawberry plants and raspberry canes giving the fields the texture of corduroy. Myths tie the production of orange marmalade to the city of Dundee, but making this and other jams was, as throughout rural Britain, a seasonal kaleidoscope of fruit preserving for winter. And the heather moorland so carefully managed for grouse produces a phenomenal quantity of thick, perfumed honey.

The great houses and castles grew many vegetables in their walled gardens for the cooks and chefs in their kitchens. Cottagers had kail yards (garden patches) whose name suggests a heavy reliance on members of the cabbage family. The Scots are not, on the whole, noted for vegetable dishes. This lack may be more apparent than real as Scottish cookery includes several soups, such as hotch-potch, which use large quantities of vegetables, delicious when well made.

The distinctive and varied foods of Scottish traditional cookery reflect this beautiful but challenging landscape, and cookery methods which relied, in many places, on the slow gentle heat of peat fires. At their best, rooted in the rural traditions of farmstead, dairy and big house, using excellent local ingredients, they are very good indeed.

*Highland cow
on moorland.*

Hazelnut Tarts

A few hectares of hazelnut 'plats' (traditional nut orchards) survive in Kent. The recipe is an 'autumn' one from one of Nell Heaton's delightful books, *A Calendar of Country Recipes* (1950).

Grind the hazelnuts, without removing their skins, in a food processor until they are mostly reduced to powder but a few larger pieces are left. Mix with the candied peel and the egg whites, lightly beaten.

Put the sugar in a small pan and add the water. Bring to the boil, stirring all the time. Add this syrup to the hazelnut mixture and stir well.

Roll the pastry out thinly and cut into 30–36 rounds, rerolling the scraps as necessary. Put them in patty tins and add a spoonful of hazelnut mixture to each case. Bake at 200°C, 400°F, Gas mark 6 for 5 minutes, then lower the heat to 180°C, 350°F, Gas mark 4 for another 10 minutes.

MAKES ABOUT 30

100g (3½oz) hazelnuts
60g (2oz) mixed candied peel, finely chopped
2 egg whites
100g (3½oz) caster sugar
3 tablespoons water
400g (14oz) puff pastry

Maids of Honour

No one really knows how these little cheesecakes acquired their name. This is a late 19th-century recipe associated with Richmond, immediately west of London.

The day before you want to bake the cakes, heat the milk to blood temperature, stir in a pinch of salt and add rennet as directed on the packet. When the curd has set and cooled, transfer it to a clean square of muslin, tie, hang over a bowl and allow the whey to drip out overnight.

Next day, rub the curd through a sieve with the butter. Beat in the egg yolks and brandy then stir in the almonds, sugar, cinnamon and the lemon juice and zest.

Roll the pastry out very thinly and cut into rounds with a plain cutter. Using a fork, lightly prick the centres of the rounds a few times, otherwise your maids may go head-over-heels in the oven.

Line patty tins with the pastry and put a generous teaspoon of mixture in each. Scatter a few currants on top of each one. Bake at 220°C, 425°F, Gas mark 7 for 7 minutes, or until the pastry is risen and nicely browned. Best eaten warm from the oven.

MAKES ABOUT 24

500ml (18fl oz) whole milk
pinch of salt
rennet
100g (3½oz) butter, at
   room temperature
2 egg yolks
1 dessertspoon brandy
12 almonds, blanched
   and chopped
30g (1oz) sugar
1 teaspoon ground cinnamon
grated zest and juice of ½ a lemon
200g (7oz) puff pastry
4 tablespoons currants

Curd Tart

On farms this Yorkshire recipe was made using 'beestings' – the first milk a cow gives after calving, which curdles naturally when heated. This is unobtainable unless you happen to have a dairy herd. Alternative methods for making curd include heating milk with eggs or Epsom salts or using rennet, the method given here.

The night before you want to make the tart, heat the milk to blood temperature and add the rennet. When the curd has set and cooled, put it into a square of clean muslin and hang above a bowl to drain overnight. It must be well drained. The next day, roll out the pastry and use it to line the tin.

Cream the butter, sugar and lemon zest together. Beat in the egg. Mash the curd with a fork, and stir into the mixture. Add the currants, peel and rum, and pour into the pastry case. Bake at 190°C, 375°F, Gas mark 5 for 40 minutes or until the filling is set.

Grate a little nutmeg over while it is still warm.

1 litre (1¾ pints) whole milk
rennet
½ quantity shortcrust pastry made with butter (see page 13)
50g (1¾oz) butter
100g (3½oz) caster sugar
grated zest of 1 lemon
1 egg
50g (1¾oz) currants
50g (1½oz) mixed candied peel
1 tablespoon rum
nutmeg

You will need a 20cm (8in) round pie dish or tart tin

Mint Pasty

A Yorkshire variation on the tradition of pastry and currants, which recurs in English baking.

Roll the pastry into a thin round a bit larger than a dinner plate and place it on a baking tray.

Cover half of it with the currants, raisins and peel. Sprinkle a little allspice over. Put the chopped mint leaves on top, scatter with brown sugar and dot with butter.

Wet the edges of the pastry, fold the other half over and pinch firmly to seal. Trim neatly. Bake at 200°C, 400°F, Gas mark 6 for 20 minutes. Best eaten soon after baking, while the scent of mint permeates the warm filling.

MAKES 1 PASTY

1 quantity shortcrust pastry made with butter and lard mixed (see page 13)
100g (3½oz) currants
50g (1¾oz) raisins
50g (1¾oz) mixed candied peel, chopped
pinch of ground allspice
2 bunches fresh mint, leaves only, finely chopped
2 tablespoons soft light brown sugar
15–25g (½–1oz) butter

Kathleen's Cornish Fairings

Sara Paston-Williams quoted this recipe from Kathleen Stevens, who worked as a maid at Lanhydrock in Cornwall, in *Good Old-Fashioned Jams, Preserves and Chutneys.*

In a large pan, melt the syrup and butter together over a low heat. Remove from the heat and stir in the sugar. Sift the flour, bicarbonate of soda and ginger together into the pan, then stir together to form a dough.

Roll into small balls, each the size of a walnut, and place on greased baking trays, leaving plenty of room between each one, as they spread during cooking.

Bake at 180°C, 350°F, Gas mark 4 for 10 minutes or until golden brown and well spread. Leave to cool on the trays for a few minutes, then transfer to a wire rack to cool completely. Store in an airtight container.

2 tablespoons golden syrup
225g (8oz) butter
175g (6oz) caster sugar
350g (12oz) self-raising flour
1 teaspoon bicarbonate
   of soda
2 teaspoons ground ginger

Honiton Fairings

Also known as brandy snaps, these thin crisp Devonshire biscuits were associated with several other fairs in southern England. Eat alone, fill with whipped cream, or serve with creamy desserts.

Put the butter, sugar and syrup in a pan and melt over a low heat. When liquid, stir in the flour, ginger, lemon juice and brandy.

Drop teaspoons of the mixture, widely spaced – the biscuits spread as they cook – on non-stick baking trays or trays lined with baking paper. Cook at 190°C, 375°F, Gas mark 5 for about 5 minutes. Remove from the oven, leave on the trays to cool for a minute, then lift each biscuit with a palette knife and wrap round the handle of a wooden spoon. If the biscuits cool too much, they can be returned to the oven for a moment to soften; or they may be left flat. When fully cooled, store in an airtight container.

MAKES 15

50g (1oz) butter
50g (1oz) demerara sugar
50g (1oz) golden syrup
50g (1oz) plain flour
½ teaspoon ground ginger
1 teaspoon lemon juice
1–2 teaspoons brandy

Ginger Biscuit Mixture for Parkin Pigs

Another recipe from Littondale in Yorkshire (see page 236). Around 5th November, this type of mixture was used for making ginger pigs, which were always known as parkin pigs in Yorkshire.

Put the sugar, butter and syrup in a pan and set them over a low heat. Mix the flour, bicarbonate of soda, baking powder and ginger in a bowl. When the butter and syrup mixture is melted, add to the dry ingredients and stir well. Add a little milk, just enough to make a coherent dough. Dust a work surface with flour and roll out to a thickness of 5mm (¼in). Cut into pig shapes, giving each one a currant eye. Bake on greased baking trays at 180°C, 350°F, Gas mark 4 for about 8 minutes (keep an eye on them, they scorch easily). Allow to cool a little before removing them with a spatula to a wire rack.

Alternatively use a round cutter to make conventional biscuits.

MAKES AROUND
25 PARKIN PIGS OR
50 CONVENTIONAL BISCUITS

120g (4oz) granulated sugar
60g (2oz) butter
120g (4oz) golden syrup
250g (9oz) plain flour, plus
     extra for dusting
1 teaspoon bicarbonate
     of soda
½ teaspoon baking powder
1 teaspoon ground ginger
1–2 tablespoons milk
currants

Oatmeal Parkin

Parkin is a north-country name for ginger breads. There are probably as many recipes for parkin as there are cooks who bake it. It comes in several types – cake-like, biscuit-like or made with oatmeal. This 1930s recipe from the Knaresborough area in Yorkshire is unusual and probably old-fashioned even then as it is based completely on oatmeal (most recipes require some flour) and includes rum.

Mix the first four ingredients together in a large bowl. Warm the syrup with the lard and butter until the fats have melted, then stir in the rum and cream. Pour onto the oatmeal mixture and stir very well. Drop the parkin mix into the tin and bake at 150°C, 300°F, Gas mark 2 for around 1½ hours, until the mixture feels set in the middle and is just starting to pull away from the edges of the tin. Cool in the tin, cut into 24 pieces and lift out, sliding a spatula underneath. Parkin should be kept covered but not airtight for a couple of days before eating.

MAKES 24

500g (1lb 2oz) medium oatmeal
¼ teaspoon salt
½ teaspoon bicarbonate of soda
2 teaspoons ground ginger
500g (1lb 2oz) golden syrup
30g (1oz) lard
30g (1oz) butter
3 tablespoons rum
1 tablespoon single cream

You will need an old-fashioned, 24cm (9½in) square Yorkshire pudding tin, 5cm (2in) deep, or similar. Grease it well with lard or butter.

Gingerbread

A very good recipe collected in central Wales in the 1930s. The use of sour cream and the mixture of spices seem more Germanic or North American than British, but many households, farms included, acquired recipes from elsewhere via friends or family members who had gone into service or migrated to the colonies and sent home novel recipes.

Cream the butter and sugar together. Warm the syrup and beat into the mixture along with the egg yolk. Mix the bicarbonate of soda with a tablespoon of boiling water and stir in. Add the raisins, peel and sour cream, and mix in the flour, baking powder and spices. Whisk the egg whites to a stiff froth and fold in, making sure everything is well mixed. Put the mixture in the cake tin and bake at 170°C, 325°F, Gas mark 3 for 1¼–1½ hours. Turn onto a cake rack to cool. Store in a tin.

120g (4oz) butter
120g (4oz) caster sugar
80g (3oz) golden syrup
1 whole egg, separated, and
  1 egg white
1 teaspoon bicarbonate
  of soda
120g (4oz) raisins
60g (2oz) mixed candied
  peel, chopped
75ml (3fl oz) sour cream
250g (9oz) plain flour
1 teaspoon baking powder
½ teaspoon ground ginger
½ teaspoon ground cinnamon
½ teaspoon ground cloves

You will need a shallow 22cm (8½in) square cake tin

Grasmere Gingerbread

Grasmere gingerbread is sold from a little shop in this Lake District village. It is very delicious and the shop recipe is a secret. This version comes from Marion Hayton.

Rub the butter into the flour. Add the other dry ingredients and mix well. Add the syrup and rub into the mixture until it is crumbly. Grease a baking sheet and press the mixture onto it in a block 1cm (½in) thick. Don't be alarmed if it's crumbly. Bake at 150°C, 300°F, Gas mark 2 until golden brown. Sprinkle with a little granulated sugar. Allow to cool for 15 minutes, then cut into fingers.

MAKES 16 FINGERS

225g (8oz) butter, plus
   extra for greasing
450g (1lb) plain flour
225g (8oz) light brown sugar
1 teaspoon bicarbonate
   of soda
1 teaspoon cream of tartar
2 teaspoons ground ginger
pinch of salt
1 tablespoon golden syrup
granulated sugar to finish

Staffordshire Fruitcake

One of the many variations of fruit cake found across Britain.

Mix the currants, peel, ground almonds and 2 tablespoons of the flour together and set aside. Beat the butter and sugar together until light and pale. Beat in the eggs, one by one, alternating each with a tablespoon of flour. When all the flour has been added, warm the treacle and stir in with the brandy, mace, lemon zest and the baking powder. Add a little milk if the mixture seems very dry. Finally, stir in the fruit mixture.

Drop into the prepared cake tin, level the top and bake at 170°C, 325°F, Gas mark 3 for 2½ hours. This cake is better if allowed to mature for a couple of weeks before cutting.

450g (1lb) currants
225g (8oz) mixed candied
 peel, chopped
120g (4oz) ground almonds
225g (8oz) plain flour
150g (5oz) butter
150g (5oz) caster sugar
4 eggs
1 tablespoon black treacle
75ml (2½fl oz) brandy
1 teaspoon ground mace
grated zest of 1 lemon
1 teaspoon baking powder
1–2 tablespoons milk

You will need a 22cm (8½in)
round cake tin, lined with
greaseproof paper

Mrs Ellis's Shearing Cake

Mrs Ellis, who lives in north Wales, makes this cake every year at sheep-shearing time. She says: 'It was handed down to me from my mother and my grandmother, and it has also been put in Katherine Hepburn's *Stories of My Life*. She was filming at our farm in *The Corn is Green* (1979) and they were doing the tea party scene in the garden and wanted a cake. I was asked if I had a cake, and I gave them my shearing cake, as we were going to shear the sheep the next day. They took it, but ate the lot and I had to make another one. The following day, Katherine Hepburn came to chat, as she often did because she was using our spare bedroom to change her clothes, and she asked if she could have the recipe for the cake as she enjoyed it so much. I wrote it down for her and, blow me, it was in her book!'

Rub the butter into the flour. Stir in currants and caster sugar. Add the eggs and milk and stir well to make a soft, but not runny mixture. Place in the cake tin. Sprinkle the top of the cake with the brown sugar.

Bake at 200°C, 400°F, Gas mark 6 for 15 minutes, then reduce the heat to 170°C, 325°F, Gas mark 3 and bake for another 1¾ hours. Test with a skewer – when the cake is cooked the skewer will come out clean. Cool in the tin.

350g (12oz) butter
450g (1lb) self-raising flour
350g (12oz) currants
350g (12oz) caster sugar
2 eggs
200ml (7fl oz) milk
1 tablespoon soft brown sugar

You will need a 22cm (9in) round cake tin, well greased and lined with greaseproof paper

Apple Cake

Apple cakes frequently feature in books of Dorset and Somerset recipes. They are eaten warm, spread with butter or served with custard or cream. This version has been re-worked to emphasise the presence of the apples. Use a well-flavoured dessert apple.

Cream the butter and sugar together until light and fluffy. Beat in the eggs. Sift the flour, salt and cinnamon together and add this to the creamed mixture. Add a little milk to slacken off, but don't overdo it; the mixture should be on the stiff side.

Put half the cake mixture into the tin. Level it off, then make a hollow in the middle with the back of a spoon. Mix the grated apple with a spoonful of brandy or any other fruit-based alcohol and put the mixture in the hollow. Don't let it touch the edges of the tin. Dollop the rest of the mixture over the top and smooth off, sealing the apple in the middle. Sprinkle the top with caster sugar.

Bake in a moderate oven at 190°C, 375°F, Gas mark 5 for 1 hour and 10 minutes. Serve warm with cream. The cake may be slightly puddingy in the middle, but should still taste good.

SERVES 8

150g (5oz) butter
150g (5oz) granulated sugar
2 eggs
300g (10oz) self-raising flour
½ teaspoon salt
1 teaspoon ground cinnamon
100ml (3½fl oz) milk
400–450g (14oz–1lb) apples,
 peeled and finely grated
1 tablespoon brandy or
 apple brandy
1 tablespoon caster sugar,
 ideally vanilla flavoured

You will need a 20cm (8in) cake tin, lined with non-stick baking parchment

Sponge Cake with Bilberries

Baking scones, cakes, biscuits and sometimes breads was something most farmers' wives did every week. They were most important for the evening meal, when no tea-table was complete without three or four choices – perhaps some scones, a plain fruit cake or tea bread, and a couple of plates of smaller cakes – buns made from a Victoria sponge mixture, some shortbreads, or something involving pastry and currants. At other times of day they were there as snacks for anyone who felt peckish after a bit of hard work in the fields, or to offer to visitors together with a cup of tea.

Baking was a necessity. Recipes were passed around from farm to farm, clipped from the *Farmer's Weekly* and newspapers, or gathered from cookery demonstrations organised by the Women's Institute. It was also a pleasure, an opportunity to exercise a skill and display creativity and make something that was both beautiful and delicious. Social events often closed with a tea to which everyone contributed and most people had a speciality – the moistest fruit cake, lightest meringues, crispest brandy snaps, made perfect by long practice, and perhaps a little knack never revealed to anyone outside the family.

This is a very light, fragile sponge recipe from Husthwaite in Yorkshire, recorded in a W.I. collection. It is important to beat the egg and syrup mixture for several minutes.

Put the sugar and water in a pan and stir gently over a low heat until the sugar has completely dissolved. Then bring to the boil and switch off the heat.

Break the eggs into a large bowl and begin whisking them with a hand-held electric beater. After a few seconds start adding the hot sugar syrup, pouring it in a thin stream and whisking all the time. Continue whisking for 5 minutes, after which you should have a light, very foamy mixture. Sift in the flour bit by bit, folding it in with a tablespoon. When the mixture is smooth, pour it into the prepared tin and bake at 180°C, 350°F, Gas mark 4 for 40 minutes. Test the top by pressing very lightly: it should feel firm to the touch and spring back a little, and the edges should be coming away very slightly from the sides of the tin. If in doubt, return to the oven for 5 minutes. Cool in the tin.

Carefully cut in half horizontally using a serrated knife. Fill with whipped cream and soft fruit, preferably bilberries picked from the moors in July or August and sharpened with a squeeze of lemon juice.

350g (12oz) granulated sugar
100ml (3½fl oz) water
3 whole eggs and 1 yolk
150g (5oz) plain flour sifted with ¾ teaspoon baking powder
100ml (3½fl oz) whipping cream
100g (3½oz) bilberries or other soft fruits such as raspberries or blueberries

You will need a deep 22cm (8½in) round cake tin lined with greaseproof paper, the base and sides buttered and dusted with caster sugar

Suffolk Cakes

Delicious little cakes with a fine texture, similar to French madeleines. A mid-19th century recipe from East Anglia, collected by Florence White.

Cut the butter into cubes, put in a mixing bowl and set in a warm place to soften. Keep working it until it is very soft and creamy.

Separate the eggs. Beat the whites to a stiff froth, then beat the yolks well. Stir the yolks into the whites and beat in the sugar and lemon zest. Gradually beat the egg mixture into the warmed butter (an electric hand beater is best for this). Be careful it doesn't curdle. Fold in the flour.

Half-fill each hollow in the bun trays and bake at 190°C, 375°F, Gas mark 5 for about 15 minutes, checking to make sure the cakes don't burn. Lift the cakes out of the bun tins and cool on a wire rack.

MAKES 24

100g (3½oz) butter, plus
   extra for greasing
4 eggs
200g (7oz) caster sugar
finely grated zest of ½ lemon
100g (3½oz) self-raising flour,
   sifted

**You will need bun trays,
well greased**

Cumberland Girdle Cakes

A cake that belongs to a northern tradition of baking on a flat iron plate called a girdle, suspended over the fire.

Mix the flour, salt and baking powder. Rub in the butter. Mix to a dough with the milk or cream. Flour a work surface lightly and roll out the dough to a circle about 5mm (¼in) thick.

Heat the girdle or pan and grease lightly with butter. Put the cake on it and cook gently for 10–15 minutes. When golden brown underneath, turn and cook for another 5–10 minutes on the other side or until golden. Cut into squares, split and serve buttered on a hot dish.

80g (3oz) plain flour, plus
   extra for dusting
pinch of salt
generous pinch of baking powder
30g (1oz) butter, plus extra
   for greasing
75ml (2½fl oz) milk
   or thin cream

**You will need a girdle or
a large heavy frying pan**

Mary Edmund's Date Sandwich

Simple, quick and satisfying baking of this sort fills cake tins all over the country. Recipes came from all over – from family or friends, the W.I., newspapers or the back of packets, or out of people's heads – and were quickly absorbed into family traditions. This version is from the Lake District.

Break up the dates and simmer with the water for about 20–25 minutes, or until soft.

Mix the oats, flour, sugar and salt in a bowl and rub in the butter. Grease the tin and press in half the oat mixture. Spread the softened dates over the top, then scatter over the rest of the oat mixture. Level neatly. Bake at 180°C, 350°F, Gas mark 4 for 30–35 minutes.

Cut into fingers while warm, but leave in the tin until cool.

MAKES 16 FINGERS

250g (9oz) dried stoned dates
250ml (9fl oz) water
150g (5oz) rolled oats
150g (5oz) self-raising flour
150g (5oz) granulated sugar
pinch of salt
150g (5oz) butter, plus a little
    extra for greasing

You will need a Swiss roll tin

Singin' Hinnie

A cake from the Northumbrian tradition of girdle baking (see the following page for more information on traditional farmhouse cookery in this area). The results are very more-ish and a little richer than the Cumberland version on page 265).

Mix the flour, salt and baking powder. Rub in the lard and butter, stir in the currants and mix to a dough using the milk. Divide in two and roll out to rounds about 1cm (1½ in) thick. Heat a girdle or a large heavy frying pan, grease lightly with lard and put a round on to cook. Keep an eye on the heat, which needs to be fairly moderate. It may take up to 15 minutes to bake. When the underside is brown, turn and cook the other side. Split crosswise, butter well, sprinkle with brown sugar and nutmeg and eat warm.

MAKES 2 LARGE CAKES
20CM (8IN) IN DIAMETER

400g (14oz) plain flour
generous pinch of salt
1 teaspoon baking powder
100g (3½oz) lard, plus extra
    for greasing
100g (3½oz) butter
150g (5oz) currants
2–3 tablespoons milk
    to mix
butter, brown sugar and
    nutmeg for serving

You will need a girdle (iron baking
sheet) or a heavy frying pan

Farmhouse Cookery in the Borders

The idea of the Scottish Borders is now confined mostly to the strip of land between Berwick-upon-Tweed and Gretna Green, but this hasn't always been so. Until the end of the Middle Ages, all the land between Yorkshire and the southern uplands of Scotland was fought over. This is apparent in some of the architecture – the walls that surround Berwick, the houses of the village of Blanchland which all face inwards, and the occasional pele tower (a fortified house) – and in the emptiness of southern Scotland.

Northwards from Yorkshire the hills become higher, bleaker and more lonely, though the flatter land towards the coast is well inhabited. West of Newcastle, the Tyne Valley cuts through the Pennines, followed along its length by Hadrian's Wall, a physical reminder that the Romans too had problems fixing a northern boundary to their empire. To the north-east a narrow strip of flat land continues along the beautiful Northumbrian coast, past great medieval castles and the little craggy island of Lindisfarne, an important monastery and centre of learning in the early Middle Ages. From the border at Berwick, the Cheviot Hills, after which the native sheep breed of the area is named, run south-west in a diagonal line, beginning as high bare grassy slopes, but forested around Kielder Water. The land drops to sea level

again near the Solway Firth, and the Eden Valley opens to the south between the Lake District mountains and the steep western slopes of the Pennines; but in Scotland the hills roll away to the north.

The flatter land on the east coast is an area of model farms with ranges of sturdy 19th-century buildings, one of which can be viewed at Beamish as part of the Open Air Folk Museum, and rich arable land growing barley and other crops. Scattered across it are former mining communities whose traditions include an interest in competitive vegetable growing, especially giant leeks and onions. The wealthier inhabitants turned their glasshouses over to tropical fruit, as Lord Armstrong at Cragside in Northumberland. Inland, Teesdale and Weardale echo the Yorkshire Dales in their west-east orientation; north of the Tyne, the landscape is more complex. Some areas were once home to lead mining communities. Some of the highest and roughest land is heather moorland, a habitat for grouse and other game. Given the height of the hills – Cross Fell in the Pennines is almost 1,000m (3,200ft) and The Cheviot is not much lower – and the fact they lie so far north, the principal farming activity is bound to be pastoral, rearing lamb and beef. Along the coast, fishing and fish curing has always been important and remains so in places such as Lindisfarne.

Hadrian's Wall, Northumberland, looking across Cuddy's Crag from Housesteads Crag.

Jams, Preserves and Drinks

Strawberry and Redcurrant Jam

Adding some redcurrant juice to the strawberries produces a better set and intensifies the flavour without being too obvious.

500g (1lb 2oz) redcurrants
500g (1lb 2oz) strawberries
500g (1lb 2oz) granulated sugar

Begin the day before by placing the redcurrants in a pan; put the lid on and cook over a very gentle heat until they have collapsed and yielded all their juice. Remove from the heat and pour the fruit into a jelly bag with a bowl underneath to catch the juice. There should be about 200ml (7fl oz).

The next day, hull the strawberries, remove any bad bits, and rinse them; halve or quarter large ones. Place in a pan with the sugar and the redcurrant juice, and heat gently, stirring to dissolve the sugar. Once this is done, bring to the boil and cook for about 15–20 minutes. Test by dropping a teaspoonful on a chilled saucer. If the jam crinkles when lightly pushed with a finger, it's set. When the setting point is reached, pour into warm, sterilised jars and seal immediately.

Pumpkin Cream

A variation on a recipe used by my mother for dealing with marrows. Try it with pumpkins from Slindon, West Sussex.

Cube the pumpkin and put in a large pan. Add enough water to cover the base of the pan and stew gently until the pumpkin is soft and can be crushed. Add a little more water if necessary, and stir to make sure it doesn't catch. Once the pumpkin has collapsed, add the sugar, butter, orange and lemon zest and the lemon juice. Cook rapidly until the mixture is thick – about 20 minutes. Pot in hot, sterilised jars. Eat within 6 weeks.

**500g (1lb 2oz) pumpkin, peeled
and seeded weight
500g (1lb 2oz) granulated sugar
60g (2oz) butter
grated zest and juice of ½ orange
grated zest and juice of 1 lemon**

Apple Butter

This could be made from any variety of apple, but particularly crab apples. In this recipe, from Somerset, I've given a small amount. Use a preserving pan if making large amounts.

750g (1lb 10oz) apples – a
    mixture of crab apples and
    Cox's work well
500g (1lb 2oz) granulated sugar
grated zest and juice of ½ lemon

Wash the apples, quarter them and cut out any unsound bits, but don't peel. Put in a pan, add enough cold water to cover and simmer gently until soft and pulpy (this can take some time with crab apples). Sieve. Measure the pulp; the above quantity should yield about 850ml (1½ pints). Return it to the pan and cook gently for an hour until quite thick, stirring from time to time.

Add the sugar, lemon zest and juice and boil rapidly until thick and no longer runny, which will take about 20 minutes. Stir constantly and make sure the mixture doesn't catch and burn; you may want to wrap your hand in a tea towel, as the mixture spits as it thickens. Pour into shallow containers and cover when cold.

Gooseberry Jelly

Most gooseberries produce a russet-coloured jam or jelly. Allegedly, this method gives a green jelly, but it depends on your gooseberries and possibly their stage of ripeness. Leveller is one variety in which the juice remains green, but even with these the jam came out reddish for me, perhaps because they were too ripe. It still tastes good, though.

900g (2lb) gooseberries, topped, tailed and washed
300ml (½ pint) water
granulated sugar (see method for quantity)

Put the berries in a pan with the water. Cook gently until they collapse. Place in a jelly bag and allow to drip overnight.

The next day, measure the quantity of juice, and allow 450g (1lb) sugar per 600ml (1 pint) of juice. Put the sugar in an ovenproof dish and place it in a warm oven to heat through. Put the juice in a pan and bring to the boil, and then cook gently for about 10 minutes. Add the hot sugar, stir to dissolve, and bring to the boil. Start testing for setting point fairly soon afterwards (see page 272). Skim, then pot in warm, sterilised jars and seal.

Pear and Ginger Jam

Pears grow well in the southern counties of the Marches, the area covering the boundary between England and Wales (see the following page for more on farmhouse produce from the Marches). Elsewhere, a tree of hard cooking pears was often planted next to farmhouses, for jams and pickles.

1kg (2¼lb) cooking pears,
  peeled, cored and chopped
10g (¼oz) fresh root
  ginger, shredded
450ml (¾ pint) water
grated zest and juice of 1 lemon
800g (1lb 12oz) granulated sugar

Put the pears, ginger and water in a pan and add the juice and zest of the lemon. Stew gently until the pears are soft. Measure the contents of the pan and add 500g (1lb 2oz) sugar per 500ml (18fl oz) pear mixture. Boil until setting point is reached (see page 272), then pot in warm, sterilised jars and seal.

Farmhouse Cookery in the Marches

The Marches is the land along the boundary between England and Wales, running from the Bristol Channel northwards up the Wye Valley, taking in Hereford and Leominster, onwards past Shrewsbury and following the course of the river Dee to Chester. The concept is as much historical as geographical. Once an important frontier, the area is littered with markers such as Offa's Dyke, which runs in a series of dots and dashes between the estuaries of the Severn and Dee, and medieval castles in various states of repair, from the splendour of Chirk to the ruins of Skenfrith. The political boundary follows a geographical one, for here the generally flat western extremity of the English Midlands meets the Welsh mountains. The hills are never far away, getting higher to the west. In the southernmost part, the river Wye loops through them in a deep, enclosed gorge, and they close in around the pretty town of Ludlow. The rocky fingers of the Long Mynd and Wenlock Edge reach north-east towards Shrewsbury and the Cheshire plain. To the east, the scenery is not entirely level; the grassy, undulating ridge of the Malverns, the sharp cone of the Wrekin and the Peckforton Hills south of Chester add variety to this flatter landscape.

However much this area may have been fought over in the past, it is now tranquil and the lower parts are domesticated and very appealing. It is a countryside of mixed farming, with pasture and meadow and some cultivated land and, in the southern part at least, orchards (see previous page for a recipe using traditional Marches orchard ingredients). It feels timeless and deeply rural.

In the northern part of the Marches, Shropshire and Cheshire have been dairy counties for centuries. The area has a mild, damp climate which produces excellent pasture; the salt deposits which lie deep below the Cheshire plain are said to give a distinctive flavour to the milk of cattle grazed here and, in turn, to contribute to the excellence of true Cheshire cheese. The importance of dairying is acknowledged in the form of the Nantwich Cheese Show, at which British cheeses in all their variety are displayed. Cattle are important over much of the rest of the Marches, either for milk or beef. Of the latter, Herefords with their copper flanks and white heads were developed in the late 18th and early 19th century in the county from which they take their name. Beef cattle and sheep become increasingly important in the western part as the hills become higher and the climate more challenging. The area also developed its own native sheep breed, named after the little town of Clun, which is buried in the hills close to the Welsh border. Another source of meat represented on National Trust land in this area is deer. They were once the exclusive preserve of the aristocracy, including the marcher lords whose ruined castles still dominate some of the towns.

Herefordshire, protected from the worst of the rain by the Black Mountains to the west, provides some especially pleasing landscapes of half-timbered buildings (as seen at Cwmmau Farmhouse) among orchards. Apples and pears were grown for dessert fruit, cooking and for drinks. Cider is as important here as it is in the South West, and the county is a centre of perry-making, a pleasant drink when not over-industrialised. Hertfordshire also grows a major part of the British blackcurrant crop, used both for desserts and cordials, and hops are grown in the Teme Valley. It is stretching things to say that the Marches include the Vale of Evesham, on the eastern side of the Severn, but the tradition of fruit growing continues here with apples, pears and plums in Worcestershire. Asparagus was a famous crop of this area, but is sadly less important than it used to be. Other fruit of local importance include damsons in Shropshire, and gooseberries (whose significance extends beyond jam to the cut-throat competitions of the Cheshire gooseberry shows).

The general cookery tradition echoes that of England as a whole, and local specialities recorded in the past seem a little neglected. Shrewsbury Cakes, so well known in the 17th century that Congreve could say someone was 'as short as a Shrewsbury cake', seem to have been forgotten in the town.

Ashes Hollow, Long Mynd, in Shropshire.

Lemon Curd

A preserve made in most farmhouse kitchens when eggs and butter were plentiful.

In the top half of a double boiler mix the sugar, butter and lemon zest and juice. Cook over boiling water, stirring from time to time, until the butter has melted and the sugar crystals dissolved. Mix in the eggs and continue to cook, stirring constantly, until the mixture thickens – about 82°C (179°F) on a jam thermometer. Pot in warm, sterilised jars and store in the fridge. Use within 6 weeks.

450g (1lb) caster sugar
100g (3½oz) unsalted butter
grated zest and juice of 2 lemons
3 eggs, beaten and strained

Marmalade

Orange marmalade became something of a Scottish speciality, both made at home and commercialised by Keiller's of Dundee. Was it something to do with the cheerful colour and the delicious smell it makes in the house during the chill dark days of January? The formula below is based on one of the numerous recipes for marmalade given in a collection of Scottish recipes in the *Scottish Women's Rural Institute Cookery Book*. It makes a transparent jelly marmalade with a generous quantity of 'chips' of orange peel suspended in it.

Seville (bitter, or marmalade) oranges
lemons (unwaxed)
granulated sugar
water

Weigh the oranges, and for every 1kg (about 2lb) of oranges, add 1 lemon to the scale pan. Make a note of the total weight of fruit. During the final boiling, you will need the equivalent weight of sugar, and half the weight of water.

Wash the fruit, put it (whole) into a large pan and cover with water. Bring to the boil and simmer gently until soft. Test from time to time (the old test was to try to push the head of a pin though the skin – if this was easy, then the fruit was done). Lemons soften quicker than oranges, and the time the latter take will vary. Remove them individually to a bowl as they soften enough. Discard the cooking water.

Cut the fruit in half and scrape out the pulp into a jelly bag and allow all the juice to run through. Squeeze the bag to collect as much juice as possible, then discard the pulp (or cook it with an equal weight of sugar to make a paste marmalade). Cut the skins of the fruit into thin slivers. Put these and the juice into a jam pan, add the sugar and water weighed according to the original weight of fruit and bring to the boil, stirring until all the sugar has dissolved. Cook rapidly to setting point, testing after about 15 minutes (see page 272).

Pot in warm, sterilised jars, cover and seal when cold.

Blackberry Curd

A delicious preserve from Wales, based on the same principle as lemon curd (see page 280).

Simmer the blackberries and the peeled, cored apple in just enough water to cover, until soft. Sieve and put the juice in a double boiler. Add the lemon juice, sugar and butter and stir over heat until the sugar dissolves. Beat the eggs and stir these in. Cook gently until the mixture thickens. Pot in warm, sterilised jars and store in the fridge. Eat within 6 weeks.

500g (1lb 2oz) blackberries
150g (5oz) apple, peeled
  and cored
juice of 1 lemon
600g (1¼lb) granulated sugar
100g (3½oz) unsalted butter
3 eggs, beaten

Marrow, Tomato and Date Chutney

Like baking, making jams and pickles was an essential part of farm life. There was always someone with a glut of fruit or vegetables, so even if individuals lacked gardens or orchards, the chances were one of the neighbours would have apples or pears or vegetable marrows to give away. In some areas, such as those close to the moorlands of the Welsh Borders, Yorkshire and parts of Scotland, country people also knew if wild fruit, such as bilberries (also known as whortleberries or whinberries) could be found growing nearby and would often take the trouble to collect it if they had time. And everyone picked blackberries.

Consequently the preserving pan was often in use, and a really enthusiastic jam-maker could produce something from almost every month of the year, making marmalade and lemon curd in late winter when citrus fruit was cheap, using rhubarb and gooseberries in late spring, and apple butter and mincemeat for Christmas mince pies in the late autumn, after the first flush of berries and orchard fruit had passed.

Pickles, too, were much appreciated, both as a method for preserving fruit and vegetables, and for the flavours they added to the cold meat, cheeses and savoury pies which often featured in farmhouse food.

1.4kg (3lb) marrow
80g (3oz) salt
900g (2lb) red tomatoes, skinned and chopped
225g (8oz) onions, chopped
350g (12oz) cooking apples, peeled, cored and sliced
600ml (1 pint) distilled malt vinegar
225g (8oz) cooking dates, stoned and chopped
450g (1lb) soft light brown sugar
1 tablespoon mustard seeds
2 tablespoons ground ginger
2 teaspoons ground allspice

**Sara Paston-Williams remarks that this
Devonshire recipe is good for using up
gluts and is excellent with beefburgers.**

Peel the marrow, cut in half, remove and discard the
seeds. Dice the flesh into 1cm (½in) cubes and layer these
in a bowl with the salt. Cover and leave for 24 hours.

Next day, rinse the salted marrow under cold running
water and drain well; set aside. Put the tomatoes, onions
and apples in a large preserving pan. Add the vinegar,
stir well, then bring to the boil. Reduce the heat and
cook gently for 30 minutes. Add the dates, sugar and
spices, followed by the marrow. Stir well and bring back
to the boil. Reduce the heat and simmer for 1½–2 hours
until thick, stirring occasionally to prevent sticking. Pour
into warm, sterilised jars, seal and store for 2–3 months
before eating.

Lallah's Chutney

Who Lallah was is unrecorded, but her chutney recipe lives on. Like most chutneys, it is better if left to mature for a few weeks before eating.

Pour the vinegar over the salt and sugar, then place in a large preserving pan with all the other ingredients. Simmer gently for 3 hours until tender. Pot in warm, sterilised jars and seal.

500ml (18fl oz) malt vinegar

40g (1½oz) salt

250g (9oz) granulated sugar

1kg (2¼lb) large apples, peeled and sliced

80g (3oz) preserved ginger in syrup, drained and sliced

60g (2oz) sultanas

30g (1oz) fresh hot chillies, seeded and chopped

1 tablespoon mustard powder

1 shallot, chopped

1 medium onion, sliced

Pickled Pears

To eat with cold meat.

Drop the prepared pears into a bowl of water with a
squeeze of lemon to prevent browning. Put the sugar,
cloves and vinegar in a large preserving pan and stir well.
Add the pears and bring to the boil. Cover and simmer
very gently until tender. Time depends on the pear variety;
underripe Williams take about 1½ hours, but hard cooking
pears may take much longer. Pot the pears and syrup in
warm, sterilised jars and seal with parchment paper.

2kg (4½lb) hard pears, peeled,
   halved and cored (use
   underripe eating pears if no
   cooking pears are available)
lemon juice
1kg (2¼lb) sugar
3 cloves
200ml (7fl oz) distilled
   malt vinegar

Red Tomato Chutney

Noted in pencil in my grandmother's cookery book, she observes with a hint of pride that it 'is very nice and like sauce,' by which I think she meant tomato ketchup. Mine is not like that but still tasty.

Mix all the ingredients in a large preserving pan. Simmer gently for about 2 hours until well reduced, thick and slightly brownish. Stir from time to time, more frequently towards the end of cooking, to make sure it doesn't stick. Pot in warm, sterilised jars and seal.

1kg (2¼lb) tomatoes, skinned and cut in small chunks
150g (5oz) onions, chopped
300g (10oz) apples, peeled, cored and chopped
300g (10oz) granulated sugar
30g (1oz) salt
½ fresh red chilli, seeds and strings removed, chopped
½ teaspoon English mustard powder
1 dessertspoon coriander seed, ground
8 allspice berries, ground
350ml (12fl oz) malt vinegar

Spiced Tomato Jelly

The original of this recipe, from *The Country Housewife's Handbook* (West Kent W.I.), was very lightly spiced, in keeping with the tastes of the mid-20th century. Add extra flavour at the end for something more robust. Excellent with cheese and cold meats.

Chop the tomatoes and put in a large preserving pan. Cook gently with the spices until soft. Sieve. Add the sugars and vinegar and bring to the boil. Add the chillies, garlic and ginger and cook gently until setting point is reached (see page 272). Pot in warm, sterilised jars and seal.

1.5kg (3¼lb) ripe tomatoes
6 cloves
½ stick cinnamon
500g (1lb 2oz) preserving sugar (which has added pectin, specially for jam-making)
1kg (2¼lb) granulated sugar
850ml (1½ pints) water
150ml (¼ pint) white wine vinegar
2 red chillies, seeds and strings removed, cut into tiny dice
3 garlic cloves, sliced into paper-thin rounds
3cm (1¼in) fresh root ginger, peeled and finely shredded

Mint Chutney

Mint sauce with a difference; the chilli and vinegar combination is good, especially after a few weeks mellowing. This recipe would have appealed to my grandfather's generation.

Put all the ingredients in a wide-mouthed jar, stirring well. Cork and leave on a sunny windowsill for 2 weeks, shaking occasionally. It keeps well in the fridge. Serve with roast lamb.

50g (1¾oz) mint leaves,
   finely chopped
150ml (¼ pint) cider vinegar
50g (1¾oz) granulated sugar
1 garlic clove, cut into slivers
1 green chilli, cut in half

Damson Pickle

A common use for damsons in the Lake District is to pickle them, for eating with cheese or cold mutton. Here is one among many recipes.

Prick the damsons all over with a darning needle and put them in a bowl. Boil the vinegar, sugar and spices together and pour over the fruit. Cover and leave overnight.

Next day, drain and reserve the liquid and re-boil. Pour over the fruit again and leave for a second night. Repeat this the next day.

On the final day, boil the fruit and the liquid gently for 5 minutes. Try not to let the skins break. Pot in warm, sterilised jars, seal and keep for at least a month before eating, preferably longer.

700g (1½lb) damsons, washed and dried
600ml (1 pint) vinegar (malt or distilled malt)
350g (12oz) granulated sugar
2–3 cloves
1 small stick of cinnamon
1 blade of mace

Elderflower Cordial

Until about 1990, if you wanted elderflower cordial you had to make it yourself. I still think homemade cordial tastes better than the commercial versions, but the elderflowers must be gathered on a dry day and used immediately or they develop an unpleasant smell.

Put all the ingredients in a large pan and stir periodically for 24 hours. Strain and pour into sterilised bottles. For use, dilute to taste.

20 heads elderflower in
   full blossom
1.6kg (3½lb) granulated sugar
1.6 litres (2¾ pints) water,
   boiled and cooled
60g (2oz) tartaric acid
2 lemons, sliced
2 oranges, sliced

Blackcurrant Liqueur

Blackcurrants became a field crop in Herefordshire for manufacturing soft drinks. This is an alcoholic version for grown-ups.

Steep all the ingredients together for 6 weeks, strain and bottle. Excellent.

300ml (½ pint) gin
350g (12oz) blackcurrants
175g (6oz) sugar
2 cloves

Kentish Cordial

A recipe from *The Country Housewife's Handbook*, good in winter and for comforting sore throats.

Stone the damsons, retaining a dozen stones. Crack these to reveal the kernels, and add to the fruit. Pour the water over the damsons and leave for 24 hours. Bring to the boil and simmer for 15 minutes. Strain and pour the hot liquor over the elderberries. Leave for 24 hours, then bring to the boil. Simmer for 10 minutes, strain and add the sugar. Add the cloves and stir in 1 teaspoon of clear honey per 500ml (18fl oz). Leave until cold, then pour into sterilised bottles.

400g (14oz) damsons
500ml (18fl oz) boiling water
175g (6oz) elderberries, about 10 heads
1kg (2¼lb) granulated sugar
2–3 cloves
clear honey

Lemon Refresher Cordial

A recipe from the Young family, National Trust tenants in Hampshire. This is a soft drink of the type that was often made for hay-making, a season of hot, back-breaking work, now almost vanished, as many farmers opt for making silage.

900g (2lb) granulated sugar
700ml (1¼ pints) water
2 lemons
20g (¾oz) citric acid (optional)

Put the sugar and water in a large pan. Add the grated zest and juice of the lemons and stir until the sugar has dissolved. Slowly bring to the boil, and the moment it reaches boiling point remove from the heat and allow to cool a little. Stir in the citric acid. Sieve the mixture and pour into sterilised bottles. Store in a cool place. Dilute to taste with cold water and serve with ice.

Citric acid helps preserve the cordial and heightens the acidity. It's easily available from a pharmacy. If the mixture is to be used quickly, the citric acid is not strictly necessary.

Strawberry Cider

A delicious summer drink commonly found in the Wessex area. Use a well-made farmhouse cider.

Crush the strawberries lightly. Place in a large bowl or jug. Scatter over the sugar and squeeze in the juice of the orange. Leave to macerate for an hour. Fill up with cider, add some ice and serve.

500g (about 1lb) strawberries
2 tablespoons caster sugar
juice of 1 orange
500ml (about 1 pint) sweet
   cider, chilled
ice

Buttered Walnuts

Most farmers' wives made simple sweets from time to time. This recipe is in honour of Wimpole Hall in Cambridgeshire, a National Trust property which holds trees belonging to the National Walnut Collection.

250g (9oz) granulated sugar
40g (1½oz) butter
100ml (3½fl oz) water
pinch of cream of tartar or
    1 teaspoon lemon juice
100g (3½oz) walnut halves
1 lime

Put the sugar, butter and water in a heavy pan and melt together over a low heat. Stir until all the sugar crystals have dissolved, then boil without stirring to 154°C (309°F) on a sugar thermometer. When a little of the mixture dropped in a bowl of cold water hardens instantly and breaks when you try to bend it, add the cream of tartar or the lemon juice. Remove the pan from the heat and dip the base in a bowl of cold water to prevent further cooking. Be careful, because the mixture is very hot.

Drop each walnut half into the hot sugar, flip over to coat and remove with a fork. Put a sheet of baking parchment or an oiled plate to cool. When cold, pack in an airtight container with sheets of baking parchment between the layers.

Cyflaith (Welsh Toffee)

Toffee-pulls were a Christmas tradition in north Wales. Family and friends would gather in an evening to socialise and make toffee. These may be a thing of the past, but making simple sweets was often an activity of farmhouse kitchens.

Put all the ingredients in a large saucepan over a low heat, stirring until all the sugar has dissolved. Increase the heat and boil fairly briskly. After 10 minutes, test by dropping a teaspoon of the mixture into cold water. If it hardens at once, the mixture is ready. Pour it immediately onto the slab or tray.

Butter both hands and (cautiously) begin to pull the mixture into strands. Initially it will be very hot and, while a skin forms on the surface, the centre retains its heat more. As it cools, you should be able to fold and stretch the mixture more intensively, giving long golden strands of toffee. Cut into small pieces while still warm; store in an airtight container.

500g (about 1lb) black treacle
500g (about 1lb) demerara sugar
120g (4oz) butter, plus extra
   for working
1 teaspoon vinegar

You will need a marble slab or large tray for working the mixture

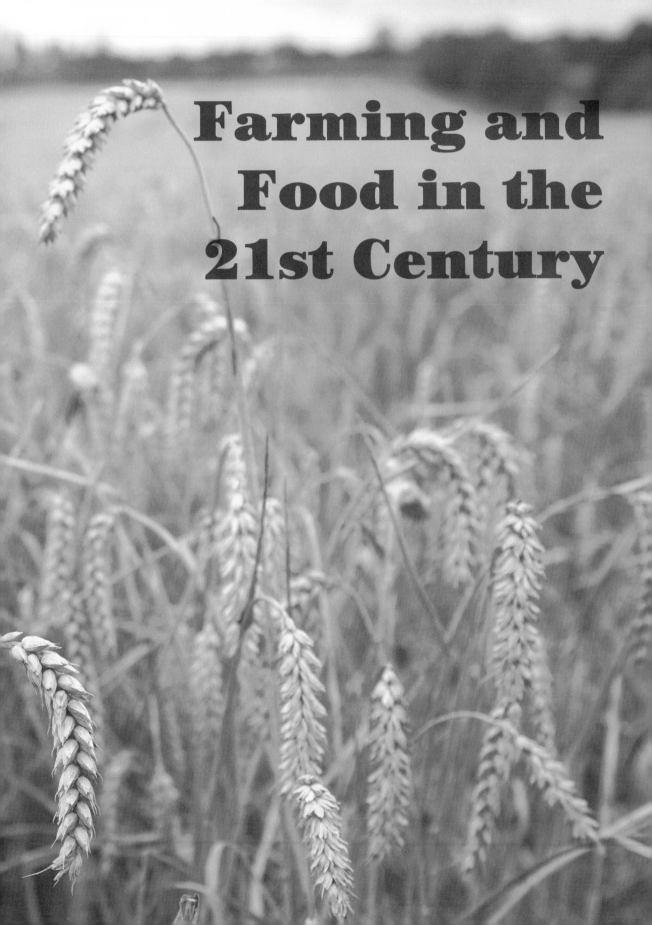

Farming and Food in the 21st Century

Appetite for Change

Food is much more than what we eat. It shapes our lives – our health and well-being, our culture, our natural environment, our security and prosperity. Food is a true measure of our approach to life itself, as individuals and as a society.

At the National Trust, we are passionate about good food – it is integral to our past, present and future. The full story of food from plot to plate is intimately represented in the places in our care, inspiring the millions of people who visit every year. Our gardeners, chefs, tenant farmers and others have daily experience of the realities of producing and preparing food in the 21st century.

The National Trust owns 250,000 hectares of land across England, Northern Ireland and Wales, more than 80 per cent of which is used to produce food, working with 1,500 tenant farmers. Food production on our land ranges from large-scale tenant-run commercial farms to kitchen gardens, allotments and orchards. Our 150 restaurants and tea-rooms serve over 8 million people every year. We have a unique perspective that spans the historic, natural, social and economic impacts of food. Over 75 per cent of Trust farms are in environmental stewardship schemes, which reward the conservation of nature and the wider environment, and provide access to the countryside. 26 of our historic kitchen gardens are in production and supply their restaurants and tea-rooms with fresh fruit and vegetables. We own over 100 traditional orchards, producing a huge variety of fruit and nuts. We grow in ways that reduce our environmental impact, with careful use of water, using peat-free compost and with minimal use of artificial chemicals. We have 145 walled gardens, many with huge potential to be restored to food production. In 2009, the National Trust launched a long-term plan to get local communities involved and handed over space for allotments to 'grow your own'. Our main aim is to help those who are new to growing to find the space they need and help them learn how and what to grow. National Trust gardeners and garden volunteers will be able to share their skills and knowledge with the community.

Previous page: Harvest time in the wheat fields surrounding Sissinghurst Castle, near Cranbrook, Kent.

Left: Newlands Valley, Cumbria.

A Recipe for Good Food

In the past, the National Trust's focus on food mainly ensured that our farmland and catering business earned money to support our charitable work. Over the years, we have developed a clearer understanding of the links between our involvement with food and our work to promote and conserve the natural and historic environment for the benefit of the nation. We are changing the way we manage our land and our business to have a much more positive impact and to invest for the future. In addition to our farms, gardens and restaurants, our open spaces provide a feast of wild food; we produce meat and crops on our land. Whether we're producing, buying, selling, cooking or talking about food, there are some basic values that matter to us. Local and seasonal food is a priority for us, but only if it is also good quality and produced sustainably. We're encouraging our tenant farmers, suppliers and individuals to join us on this journey.

In the last 15 years, the amount of land used to grow fruit and vegetables in the UK has declined by a fifth. Orchards have been destroyed and we've lost many varieties of fruit and vegetables bred and adapted over centuries. We now import around 90% of our fruit and 40% of our vegetables into the UK.

The places in the care of the National Trust have a long history of horticulture, particularly grand estates with their kitchen gardens, glass-houses and orchards. Yet over the years, many of our walled gardens have been neglected or even turned into car-parks – a clear demonstration of changing values! More recently, we've begun to realise how valuable these places are and how much we can learn from the past for the future. The National Trust has already restored many of our historic kitchen gardens and brought them back into production with the help of the local community – others will follow. We're caring for a huge variety of fruit and vegetables that might otherwise be lost forever. We've really come to appreciate the benefits of growing and eating seasonally. It helps to conserve the natural and cultural heritage of our gardens and orchards, and it brings them to life for our visitors. It is great for our chefs to serve the produce and to let their customers know that it was picked there that day. In future, we want to see more fruit and vegetables grown on National Trust land – not just in the kitchen gardens, and not just by our staff but by local people too. We want to garden in ways that improve the soil, let wildlife thrive and use a minimum of water and energy. We are responding to climate change, and the different growing conditions it is bringing, by adapting the kinds of plants that we grow and the way that we grow them.

From Plot to Plate

The whole food story, from plot to plate, is intimately represented in the places in our care and our practical experience in managing them. We are striving to produce and sell food that benefits people and the environment. A wide variety of high-quality food is produced on National Trust land and from the coast and freshwater in our care, including:

- Beef and lamb from extensively grazed grasslands
- High-quality grains for milling and brewing
- Milk and dairy from productive pastures
- Fish and seafood from healthy stocks, caught sensitively
- Fruit and vegetables grown in fields on a large scale
- Venison from wild and parkland deer
- Vegetables and fruit from kitchen gardens and orchards
- Wild food from hedgerows and woodlands

Everyone benefits from consuming the high quality food that the National Trust and our tenant farmers produce and sell, which has a clear origin and rewards high standards of production. As part of this:

- People can buy food direct from Trust farmers or close to where it was produced through local shops, pubs and markets
- Supermarket shoppers can buy food from the Trust's estate via farmers working together to supply the mass market
- Farmers and other producers receive a fair price for the food they sell
- Our chefs have the skills and knowledge to buy and cook seasonal food from local producers
- Food waste is minimised and composted
- People have access to the countryside and the places where their food is grown
- People can visit the National Trust to learn about food and get involved in growing and cooking their own
- Local communities have the space and skills to grow their own food
- Tea, coffee and other global foods are fairly traded and from a known origin

This food is produced in environmentally responsible ways, so that:

- Farming practices protect soil and water
- Wildlife habitats, landscapes and historic features are conserved
- Animal breeds and plant varieties are chosen that suit the local environment
- Animals are looked after to high welfare standards
- Energy, water, fertilisers and chemicals are used efficiently
- Waste is minimised and managed effectively

Local Food

Since the late 1990s, encouraging local food economies has received much attention. The aims include reducing 'food miles', raising awareness of local food production, and re-connecting farmers and consumers. Networks of Farmer's Markets have proved enormously popular, bringing produce directly to the public. Farm shops are also increasing attractive to shoppers wanting to know more about the food they eat and how it was reared or grown. Farm shops which rely on produce grown on the farm can also offer guarantees of quality, especially for home-produced meat.

Other methods of direct marketing have extended the reach of farm produce. The 'vegetable box', in which market gardeners or farmers deliver seasonal vegetables directly to the doorstep is a growing industry; meat can also be ordered in a similar fashion. Many farms have developed websites with information about the farm and its produce and use suitable packaging and post or courier to deliver items. The idea of the retailer is not completely ignored however, and local food shops are an important element in local food economies; interest in this and the idea of 'food mapping' to understand local purchasing patterns are increasing.

A number of National Trust tenants have set up such schemes, including Coleshill Organics near Swindon. Sonia Oliver of Coleshill describes her experience of running a successful business:

'We love being right at the heart of the community, producing fresh, great-tasting fruit and vegetables for local people. We run a weekly box scheme, go to farmers' markets and supply produce to local shops, pubs and schools, all within 25 miles of the Coleshill Estate. We have a shop in the walled garden, and our open door policy means that people can come and see the produce being grown. We had over 1,000 schoolchildren here last year, picking and eating their way around the garden! Equally important to us is growing organically – our customers really value knowing not only where their food is from but how it's been grown. We employ about 10 local people and we run apprenticeships to help new starters learn the tricks of the trade.'

View from Clunbury Hill in Shropshire, across a patchwork of fields.

At the Brockhampton Estate in Herefordshire, after the Foot and Mouth outbreak in 2001, property manager Les Rogers was looking for ways to support our tenant farmers:

'We wanted to help create farm businesses that were sustainable – not only for the environment, but for our tenants and their livelihoods. They now supply cakes to our tea-room, rear Hereford beef for local Trust restaurants and produce about 14 different jams and chutneys from the estate's fruit and vegetables! The preserves have been incredibly popular in our tea-room and shop, and other local shops are now selling them too. Thanks to this business, we've got our 100 acres of orchards back into full production after years of neglect, which is great to see.'

Farm Foods for Sale

Some of the most-visited National Trust properties are now holding regular farmers' and food markets, including Stourhead and Lacock Abbey in Wiltshire, Waddesdon Manor in Buckinghamshire, Sissinghurst in Kent and Dunster Castle in Somerset. In addition, many National Trust properties or tenants sell direct to the public via farmers' markets, locally or online. Visit www.nationaltrust.org.uk/food to find out more.

A free range hen in the fields at Low Sizergh Farm, Cumbria.

Index

Anne Horne's butter tart 172
apple butter 275
apple cake 260
apple pancakes with cider sauce 160
asparagus tartlets 40
athol brose 197
bacon and spinach pie 60
baked eggs with tarragon 35
Bakewell pudding 170
bara brith 224
barley bread 205
barley bannocks 232
barm brack 225
beef
    beef in Branscombe bitter 91
    beef, Guinness and oyster pie 88
    Bill's burgers 66
    Carlisle steak 100
    Cornish pasties 58
    jellied beef in brown ale 50
    meat and tatie pie 97
    pot roast brisket with summer
        vegetables 90
    potted beef 48
    roast beef and Yorkshire pudding
        94
    Staffordshire steaks 96
    steak and kidney pie or pudding
        92
beef in Branscombe bitter 91
beef, Guinness and oyster pie 88
Bill's burgers 66
biscuits
    ginger biscuit mixture for parkin
        pigs 253
    gingerbread (Welsh) 255
    Grasmere gingerbread 256
    Kathleen's Cornish fairings 251
    Honiton fairings 252
    Mrs Watson's iced ginger
        shortcake 239
    My lady's shortcake 242
bitter orange marmalade 281
blackberry curd 282
blackberry jelly 190
blackcurrant liqueur 294

bread and bread rolls
    bara brith 224
    barley bread 205
    barm brack 225
    Cornish splits 208
    Ellerbeck spice bread 220
    fruit loaf 222
    Honiton fairings 252
    Kathleen's Cornish fairings 251
    Kentish huffkins 207
    Norfolk rusks 235
    rye bread 204
    Sally Lunn 209
    soda farls 234
    wheaten bread 206
    wigs 212
broad bean cawl 32
brown scones 229
bubble and squeak soup 18
buttered walnuts 300
cakes
    apple cake 260
    apple pancakes with cider sauce
        160
    cherry bumpers 165
    Cornish potato cakes 142
    Cumberland girdle cake 265
    gingerbread (Welsh) 255
    Grasmere gingerbread 256
    hazelnut cake 196
    maids of honour 247
    Mary Edmund's date sandwich
        266
    Mrs Ellis's shearing cake 259
    Mrs Watson's iced ginger
        shortcake 239
    my lady's shortcake 242
    potato and apple cake 161
    saffron cake 219
    Shrewsbury cakes 238
    singin' hinnie 267
    sponge cake with bilberries 262
    Staffordshire fruit cake 258
    strawberry shortcake 240
    Suffolk cakes 264
    teacakes 211

Cambridge cheese 200
caramelised baked pumpkin 164
Carlisle steak 100
cawl 28
celery sauce for turkey 134
champ 148
Cheddar pork pie 61
cheese, a dish of 38
cheese, Cambridge 200
cheese puddings 45
cheese tartlets 43
cherry bumpers 165
chicken and poultry
    chicken and parsley pie 110
    chicken pudding 112
    devilled chicken 108
    roast goose with sage and onion
        stuffing 118
    salt duck 120
    smothered chicken 62
    turkey escalopes with lemon and
        thyme 114
chicken and parsley pie 110
chicken pudding 112
chutneys
    Lallah's chutney 286
    marrow, tomato and date
        chutney 284
    mint chutney 291
    red tomato chutney 288
clotted cream and blackberry ripple
    ice 180
Cornish fish pie 69
Cornish pasties 58
Cornish potato cakes 142
Cornish splits 208
crempog 218
cream scones 230
Cumberland clipping time pudding
    176
Cumberland girdle cake 265
Cumberland sausage in beer 104
curd tart 248
cyflaith 301
damson pickle 292
damson sauce 194

Denise Bell's slow roast shoulder of pork 102
desserts
    Anne Horne's butter tart 172
    Bakewell pudding 170
    clotted cream and blackberry ripple ice 180
    Cumberland clipping time pudding 176
    curd tart 248
    Devon whitepot 167
    gingerbread crumble 178
    gooseberries with elderflower zabaglione 188
    hazelnut tarts 246
    junket 199
    Mrs Palmer's Russian cream 182
    Oldbury gooseberry pies 187
    pear tarts 162
    plums and cream 187
    raspberry cream 183
    rhubarb and ginger fool 192
    spiced plum tart 195
    Snowdon pudding 177
    stewed pears 186
    Sutton wakes puddings 166
    treacle custard tart 173
    treacle tart 174
devilled chicken 108
Devon scones 228
Devon whitepot 167
Devonshire stew 145
a dish of cheese 38
drinks
    blackcurrant liqueur 294
    elderflower cordial 293
    Kentish cordial 296
    lemon refresher cordial 297
    strawberry cider 298
dumplings, Norfolk 124
elderflower cordial 293
eggs
    baked eggs with tarragon 35
    Nikki Exton's duck egg frittata with spinach and butternut squash 34
Ellerbeck spice bread 220
escalopes of pork with apples and cider 101
ffagod 129
fish pie, Cornish 69
Franklin's potatoes 144

fruit loaf 222
game
    game pie 56
    hare soup 25
    hare stew 122
    partridge pudding 115
    venison bourguignon 124
    venison sauce 141
    wood-pigeon stew 121
game pie 56
Gillian Temple's Herdwick tatie pot 81
ginger biscuit mixture for parkin pigs 253
gingerbread (Welsh) 255
gingerbread crumble 178
goose, roast with sage and onion stuffing 118
gooseberries with elderflower zabaglione 188
gooseberry jelly 276
Grasmere gingerbread 256
green pea soup 21
grouse pie 65
Hadrian's Wall lamb with root vegetables 76
ham cooked in cider 53
ham loaf 49
hare soup 25
hare stew 122
hatted kit 198
hazelnut cake 196
hazelnut tarts 246
Honiton fairings 252
hotch-potch 27
Ice, clotted cream and blackberry ripple 180
Irish stew 85
jams, jellies and preserves
    blackberry curd 282
    blackberry jelly 190
    gooseberry jelly 276
    lemon curd 280
    pear and ginger jam 277
    pumpkin cream 274
    spiced tomato jelly 290
    strawberry and redcurrant jam 272
jellied beef in brown ale 50
jugged peas 149
Julia Horner's cushion of lamb 74
junket 199
kailkenny 147

Kathleen's Cornish fairings 251
Kentish cordial 296
Kentish huffkins 207
kidneys in onions 128
Lallah's chutney 286
lamb or mutton
    Gillian Temple's Herdwick tatie pot 81
    Hadrian's Wall lamb with root vegetables 76
    Irish stew 85
    Julia Horner's cushion of lamb 74
    kidneys in onions 128
    lamb or mutton liver with oranges and tomatoes 130
    lamb or mutton rogan josh 86
    lamb steaks with quince 80
    mutton and barley broth 26
    saucer pies 68
    slow-roast Herdwick mutton with salsa verde 78
    tiesen niniod 146
    Welsh lamb, mutton and laver 84
lamb or mutton liver with oranges and tomatoes 130
lamb or mutton rogan josh 86
lamb steaks with quince 80
laver sauce 139
leek pasty 44
lemon curd 280
lemon refresher cordial 297
lentil and caraway soup 20
little cheese puddings 45
little cheese tartlets 43
maids of honour 247
marrow, tomato and date chutney 284
Mary Edmund's date sandwich 266
meat and tatie pie 97
mint chutney 291
mint pasty 250
Mrs Ellis's shearing cake 259
Mrs Ingleby's oatcakes 236
Mrs Palmer's Russian cream 186
Mrs Watson's iced ginger shortcake 239
mushrooms in cream 156
mutton and barley broth 26
my lady's shortcake 242
Nikki Exton's duck egg frittata with spinach and butternut squash 101
Norfolk dumplings 124
Norfolk rusks 235

oatcakes
    Mrs Ingleby's oatcakes 236
    Staffordshire or Derbyshire
        oatcakes 214
oatmeal, herring and nettle champ 70
oatmeal parkin 254
Oldbury gooseberry pies 187
onions with cream sauce and
    Wensleydale cheese 157
onion sauce 140
parsnip fritters 153
partridge pudding 115
pasties, Cornish 58
pear and ginger jam 277
pears, stewed 186
pear tarts 162
peas, jugged 149
pease pudding and ham 106
pickles
    damson pickle 292
    pickled pears 287
    pickled red cabbage 156
pickled pears 287
pickled red cabbage 156
pikelets 215
pitcaithy bannock 243
plums and cream 187
pork
    a Shropshire breakfast 39
    bacon and spinach pie 60
    Cheddar pork 'pie' 61
    Cumberland sausage in beer 104
    Denise Bell's slow-roast shoulder
        of pork 102
    escalopes of pork with apples and
        cider 101
    ffagod 129
    ham cooked in cider 53
    ham loaf 49
    pease pudding and ham 106
    pork pie 54
    roast pork with ginger and
        Madeira 103
    stuffed pork fillet 107
    Valerie Burke's orchard picnic loaf
        52
pork pie 54
pot roast brisket with summer
    vegetables 90
potato cakes, Cornish 142
potato case pie 63
potatoes, Franklin's 144

potato and apple cake 161
potted beef 48
pumpkin, caramelised baked 164
pumpkin cream 274
raspberry cream 183
red cabbage, pickled 156
red cabbage, stewed 152
red tomato chutney 288
rhubarb and ginger fool 192
roast beef and Yorkshire pudding 94
roast goose with sage and onion
    stuffing 118
roast pork with ginger and Madeira
    103
rye bread 204
saffron cake 219
salad sauce 134
Sally Lunn 210
salt duck 120
saucer pies 68
sauces
    celery sauce for turkey 134
    damson sauce 194
    laver sauce 139
    onion sauce 140
    salad sauce 135
    sherry or madeira sauce 177
    venison sauce 141
    watercress sauce for trout or
        salmon 136
scones, brown 229
scones, cream 230
scones, Devon 228
Shrewsbury cakes 238
a Shropshire breakfast 39
singin' hinnie 267
slow-roast Herdwick mutton with
    salsa verde 78
smoked haddock and new potato
    salad 71
smothered chicken 62
Snowdon pudding 177
soda farls 234
souffléed green pea pancakes 150
soups
    bubble and squeak soup 18
    broad bean cawl 32
    cawl 28
    green pea soup 21
    hare soup 25
    hotch-potch 27
    lentil and caraway soup 20

    mutton and barley broth 26
    spinach soup 23
    spinach and sorrel soup 22
    stilton and celery soup 24
    Ulster broth 23
spiced tomato jelly 290
spiced plum tart 195
spinach and bacon pie 60
spinach soup 23
spinach and sorrel soup 22
sponge cake with bilberries 262
Staffordshire or Derbyshire oatcakes
    214
Staffordshire fruit cake 258
Staffordshire steaks 96
steak and kidney pie or pudding 92
stewed pears 186
stewed red cabbage 152
stilton and celery soup 24
strawberry cider 298
strawberry and redcurrant jam 272
strawberry shortcake 240
stuffed pork fillet 107
Suffolk cakes 264
Sutton wakes pudding 166
sweets
    buttered walnuts 300
    cyflaith 301
teacakes 211
tiesen nionod 146
tomato tartlets 42
treacle custard tart 173
treacle tart 174
turkey escalopes with lemon and
    thyme 114
Ulster broth 33
Valerie Burke's orchard picnic loaf 52
venison bourguignon 125
venison steaks with allspice, juniper
    berries and sloe gin 126
venison sauce 141
walnuts, buttered 300
watercress butter 138
watercress sauce for trout or salmon
    136
Welsh lamb, mutton and laver 84
Welsh rarebit 46
wheaten bread 206
wigs 212
wood pigeon stew 121

Bibliography

Clark, Lady Charlotte, *The Cookery Book of Lady Clark of Tillypronie*, Southover Press (1994)

Fitzgibbon, Theodora, *A Taste of Wales*, Pan (1971)

Fitzgibbon, Theodora, *A Taste of the West Country*, Pan (1972)

Fitzgibbon, Theodora, *A Taste of the Lake District*, Pan (1980)

Freeman, Bobby, *First Catch Your Peacock*, Y Lolfa Cyfo (1996)

Grigson, Jane, *English Food*, Penguin Books (1992)

Heaton, Nell, *A Calendar of Country Receipts*, Faber and Faber (1950)

Heaton, Nell, *Traditional Recipes of the British Isles*, Faber and Faber (1951)

Heaton, Nell, *Nell Heaton's Cooking Dictionary*, Cresta Books (1953)

Hutchins, Sheila, *Your Granny's Cook Book*, Daily Express (1971)

Leyel, Mrs C. F., and Hartley, Miss Olga, *The Gentle Art of Cookery*, Chatto and Windus (1925)

McNeill, F. Marian, *The Scots Kitchen*, Blackie and Son (1963)

Paston-Williams, Sara, *Good Old-fashioned Jams, Preserves and Chutneys,* The National Trust (2008)

Tibbott, S. Minwel, *Welsh Fare*, National Museum of Wales (1976)

Uttley, Alison, *Recipes From an Old Farmhouse,* Faber and Faber Ltd (1966)

Webb, Mrs Arthur, *Farmhouse Cookery*, George Newnes and Sons (*c.*1930)

White, Florence, *Good Things in England*, Jonathan Cape (1932)

Farmer's Weekly, *Farmhouse Fare* (1950)

National Federation of Women's Institutes, *Traditional Fare of England and Wales* (1948)

West Kent Federation of Women's Institutes, *The Country Housewife's Handbook* (1943)

Yorkshire Federation of Women's Institutes, *Yorkshire Recipes* (1937)

Picture Credits